The Politics of Social Work
Research and Evaluation

edited by

Bob Broad

In association with the
Social Work Research Association

VENTURE PRESS

Published by
VENTURE PRESS
16 Kent Street
Birmingham
B5 6RD

British Library Cataloguing-in-Publication Data
A catalogue record for this book is available from the British Library

ISBN 1 86178 035 4 (paperback)

Cover design by:
Western Arts
194 Goswell Road
London
EC1V 7DT

Printed in Great Britain

Contents   page

Editor's Acknowledgements

I would first like to thank the Social Work Research Association (SWRA) and Venture Press, Birmingham (especially Christine Sedgwick) for their support for this book. In relation to the former, and at a time of constant pressure in universities, and change within the SWRA, it has been most heartening that colleagues have been prepared to offer their support and expertise. In particular a special word of thanks is extended to those members of the SWRA's executive who acted as valued readers for one or more of the book's chapters. These are: Professor Mike Fisher (National Institute of Social Work), Dr. Pat Cawson (NSPCC), Joan Orme (University of Southampton), Maria Parsons (Oxford Brookes University), Dave Allen (Warwickshire Social Services Department), Helen Gorman (University of Central England), and Imogen Taylor (University of Bristol). Without all these colleagues this book would have not been produced. Also thanks are extended to Professor Malcolm Payne (Manchester Metropolitan University) for his initial support for such a book. A further word of thanks is extended to Professor Dave Ward, Head of Department, Department of Social and Community Studies, De Montfort University Leicester, who in his usual positive way encouraged and supported, not only the SWRA, by the University hosting the successful 1996 SWRA conference held in Leicester, but also enabled me to manage and complete this project. Above all a very special thanks is extended to all the contributors for producing thought-provoking and interesting chapters of a high quality. It is also important to acknowledge that the idea for this book came from a SWRA conference with the same title, and I warmly thank all those who supported and participated in that conference.

Finally, may I take this opportunity of thanking, and probably embarrassing, Professor Colin Fletcher of the Education Research Unit, at the University of Wolverhampton for his inspired teaching of research, and his support to me and others in their research endeavours.

Chapter 1
Political dimensions in social work research and evaluation

Bob Broad

The aim of this introductory chapter is twofold; first to set out the rationale for the book and its structure and second to introduce readers to key issues connected with politics, funding, and research. It will contain an overview of the book's key themes and purpose, and establish the broader context within which funded research and evaluation in social work takes place. Particular reference will be made to the politics of research in relation to stakeholders' interests, knowledge, funding, methodologies, and equal opportunities. In that it draws on some of my own research experiences the chapter is presented from a researcher's perspective as well as that of an academic editor to a collection. This chapter also pulls together the book's key themes and lessons learnt by researchers, and highlights common concerns. The issue of whether the politics of research and evaluation in social work is a problem, challenge, or an opportunity is a central and re-emerging theme which this chapter introduces, and the book seeks to address. Furthermore, and as a result of the book's strong empirical base, it contains informed reflections on social work research practice and methods, cautionary tales as well as tips from the field. Its contribution to the field therefore lies in ethical practice and development, research policy, and grounded, applied or practice theory areas, informed by empiricism and experience.

In this book the term 'politics' is taken to mean the range of influences and structures impacting on social work research and evaluation. According to The Concise Oxford Dictionary, politics is defined as 'relating to a person's or organisation's influence or status'. In social work practice and research there is often more acknowledgement of 'role' and less of 'status.' In research the issue of stakeholders' status, in deciding on whether to fund, authorise or publish a piece of research is fundamental. In social work research and evaluation the term 'politics', and accompanying status and influence elements, can apply at the macro or micro level. The former takes account of the broader social work research context and general strategies for surviving and succeeding, including obtaining funding for research projects or researchers. The latter focuses more on practical issues, especially the ways in which individual research projects are conducted, shaped and compromised by local and internal considerations. There is a symbiotic relationship between the two levels.

In the book the term 'research' is used to describe professional supervised activities (including post-qualifying practitioner research) which produce and/or analyse information relevant to practice, delivery systems and management in social work. Whilst such activity is predominantly undertaken within university departments this is not always the case. Furthermore such research is usually conducted within established, though not always agreed upon, theoretical disciplines, methodological frameworks, and codes of conduct.

Background to the book

For those like me, who seek to understand and who always value the ways in which ideas and thoughts become translated into action, what follows is a description of the processes involved in producing this book. There are parallels here worth noting, between the genesis of this *book*, and its subsequent development and production, and a *research project*, including those processes and elements such as the selection of material for inclusion, and therefore which/whose knowledge is chosen and subsequently published.

I will first explain the origin and development of this book. Such an explanation is especially important in a book about the politics of research and evaluation, because like a research project there were many processes and reflections which have informed the final product. There are also questions about the subsequent development of the book such as how was it decided who should or would contribute? what was the editorial process? which merit some acknowledgement and discussion.

Since I joined the Social Work Research Association (SWRA) as a member, in 1991, and then an executive member, there have been regular research conferences put on by the Association. Most of these have been around the theme of involving practitioners or users in research or forming partnerships in research. Yet by 1996 and ironically despite local, ongoing and possibly expanding interest in post-qualifying practitioner research at Masters, MPhil and PhD levels, related to the next Research Assessment Exercise (RAE), the topic did not seem one which had a national constituency or network, and was not perceived as being sufficiently 'interesting' to merit a further national conference.

A fresh topic therefore was sought for the 1996 SWRA conference, and one which reflected topical developments and concerns by researchers, whether working in agencies or universities or elsewhere. The original idea for *The Politics of Social Work Research and Evaluation* came from the 1996 Social Work Research Association conference with the same title, held in Leicester and hosted by De Montfort University. The conference title reflected the concerns of SWRA executive members that the climate in which research is conducted is becoming more political, and fragmented in terms of the range of those institutions conducting social work research, as well as the types of research being undertaken. There are key funding and commissioning issues (for example, who funds and commissions research?) and questions about how research agendas are set and by whom? All of this was underpinned by a strong sense that research needed to be more aware of the emerging issues of user and carer involvement and participation in research, and of anti-discriminatory practice in research. Above all, there was a developing awareness amongst the SWRA executive, and many others, that the social work research and evaluation climate was becoming 'tougher', more demanding, more sophisticated, and more competitive. This was primarily in terms of competition for research funds, but also in terms of the sort of research expected, for example focusing more on service outcomes than resource inputs (and away from process-descriptive and/or more exploratory-investigative research) as the primary evaluative points, and on an emerging 'what works' philosophy being applied to research requirements.

In this book one important political dimension is that those most actively involved in the SWRA, and subsequently the contributors, are mostly from 'new' universities or, less so, from social care agencies. It is the case, as Mike Fisher describes in his chapter, that the RAE, rewarding with funding those universities with 'good' research performance, and punishing or effectively eliminating the research aspirations of those with a developing research record, encourages a more divisive, political, and competitive climate. In the field of social care it is also the case that, faced with financial constraints, agencies use research for more precise strategic purposes than might have previously been the case. For example, research findings can be used 'politically' as a means not only to provide a justification for the continuation of particular services but also to redefine and privatise them (on this point see Truman's chapter).

The politics of social work research and evaluation conference
The aim of the SWRA 1996 conference then, similar to this book, was to explore issues and offer opportunities to exchange ideas about the various political dimensions of research and evaluation in social work research.

In the conference's promotional literature it was stated:

> Knowledge is power and research creates knowledge. Researchers are thus in a powerful position to define social issues and to shape public responses. Researchers must therefore face up to fundamental questions

about control of the research agenda, about their independence, and about the relationship between research and the political process. In social care, research and evaluation are under pressure from different stakeholders, often with conflicting agendas. Organisations that commission research may be under pressure to use it to defend services and research reports may be subject to editorial attempts to achieve this goal. (SWRA, 1996)

In other words the conference set out to address ethical questions about the funding, conducting and publishing of social work research.

At that very well attended and lively conference the two excellent and high-profile speakers were Chris Davies, Director of Somerset Social Services, and Anna Coote, Deputy Director, Institute for Public Policy Research (IPPR). Although neither was able to write a chapter for this book their contributions on the book's political themes, especially dissemination and accessibility, are important to record here. First, Davies's comments that researchers needed to make their findings more accessible to agencies, whereas Coote's suggestion that researchers can be too precious about 'their' research and not prepared to take the risk of putting it in the public arena were especially well made. Coote gave examples of IPPR's work on rights to welfare and citizen's juries and illustrated the importance of accessing the media and argued that it is better to be heard and misunderstood than to be ignored. Davies argued that research must change from a 'push' to a 'pull' approach and that he was not in favour of researchers 'parachuting' into areas and agencies, with research agendas firmly fixed, but should work with practitioners and managers to define the research issues to be addressed, thus building on and developing existing practice.

The conference also included a broad range of workshops, and prospective workshop leaders were asked to ensure they addressed political and power issues as they affected or impacted on their research. The workshops covered topics as diverse as power issues in a peer research project about young people leaving care (subsequently published separately [Broad and Saunders, 1998]), qualitative or quantitative methods (Ian Shaw), the politics of difference (Jenny Harris and Ian Paylor), empowering users through the research process (Mark Harrison), collaboration between agency and university research (Greta Bradley and Jill Manthorpe), an evaluation of a private shopping service (Andy Beckenn and Mary Corcoran), peer-led needs assessment of the sexual health of gay men (Carole Truman), and ethnicity needs assessment (Kusminder Chahal).

All of the original 1996 workshop leaders, prospective workshop leaders, speakers from the previous year's SWRA conference, and subsequently, when other contributions were required, other SWRA members were invited to submit chapter outlines addressing one or more of the following themes or areas:

- The macro context within which social work research and evaluation are conducted
- The politics of obtaining and sustaining access to agencies and data
- Identifying the political issues for postgraduate and practitioner research students
- The politics of obtaining funding, and/or negotiating time to undertake research
- Identifying the political issues involved in publishing research findings
- The politics of involving users in social work research and evaluation
- The politics and use of performance indicators and targets
- The politics of joint agency-university involvement in research
- Anti-discriminatory research practice
- Defining the research problem(s) to be addressed. Who decides? How?
- The politics of different research and evaluation methodologies
- The Research Assessment Exercise.

It was also made clear that this edited collection would need to 'stand on its own', and in accord with Venture Press's normal high academic standards, and was not 'just' a collection of conference papers. The chapter outlines that were submitted were then presented before the executive of the Social Work Research Association for its approval. In 1998 Venture Press agreed to publish this edited collection, as part of its Social Work Research Association research series. Members of the Social Work Research Association executive acted as advisers for each of the chapters.

Funding for research
There are a limited number of prime sources of funding for research and researchers. In the areas of social work, social care, and criminal justice work these sources are: central government (especially the Department of Health and the Home Office), large specialist research bodies (for example the Economic and Social Research Council [ESRC]) and programmes (for

example the ESRC's youth-in-transition research programme), large specialist charitable trusts (for the Joseph Rowntree Foundation) local government (for example, social services departments), smaller philanthropic trusts (for example City Parochial), and voluntary organisations (for example, in the child care field, Barnardo's). There are also a range of European Union funding sources, provided through specific programmes, and usually requiring some sort of complex cross-border arrangement; this can, if successful, be in turn, rewarding in RAE terms, exhausting in personal terms, and administratively bewildering (yes – there really will be a single European currency soon). The Central Council for the Education and Training of Social Workers (or CCETSW) is also a source of limited funding associated with the training and development of social workers (see, for example, Harrison and Humphries, 1997). Funding also goes direct to notable centres of research based outside the university sector, in respect of children, the National Children's Bureau's Research Unit and, more generally, the Policy Studies Unit (although since 1998 this is has been sited within the University of Westminster). The National Institute of Social Work's Research Unit is the only Department of Health research unit not in a university. The National Lottery also funds research, and many local authorities still carry a research function, albeit, one senses, a much reduced evaluative one compared with the 1970s. Probation services are more closely scrutinised by and accountable to central government (the Home Office) than seems to be the case with local authority social services departments, and probation services collect management information for the Home Office as well as for their own uses, rather than conduct their own and separate research. A particular version of the 'what works' lobby (i.e. one which produces measurable cognitive changes in offenders) seems to be dominating probation work evaluations, to the exclusion of many other approaches and understandings.

The Association of Directors of Social Services also has an important contributory role to research in that it can authorise, access, promote, or block social work research conducted across several different local authorities. There is also the *Research in Practice* project (Association of Directors of Social Services Initiative in Dartington) focusing on a range of children and family research issues. Other regional and local research initiatives include the seeking of funding from clusters of local authorities by specific universities in order to run local research seminars, or to disseminate existing local authority research findings.

There are other more limited funding sources, within universities (through the Higher Education Funding Council or by the provision of postgraduate bursaries/grants), exceptionally through the core funding of specialist research posts, and lastly smaller funds from other miscellaneous bodies, for university staff to conduct and supervise research. Subject to satisfactory completion, postgraduate practitioner researchers at MPhil/PhD level are another source of original, and often excellent, research (see, for example the contributions contained in Broad and Fletcher [eds.], 1993).

The Department of Health is a most important funder of social work research, not necessarily in terms of the amount of moneys provided (although that can be substantial) but in terms of the perceived kudos to a university in attracting such prestigious funding. It can also provide an excellent opportunity to network (i.e. obtain further knowledge about research and future research) and influence. The downside of receiving government research is being on the receiving end of a range of obvious and subtle controls and checks. These can include formal or unstated checks on the topic or topics being researched, the university/ researcher/supervisor employed, the methods used, the findings, the tone of the report, the nature, ordering and extent of the recommendations made, its published form(s), and finally the way(s) the material is disseminated. It is well known in the social work and criminal justice fields which institutions and individuals regard themselves as 'eligible' so far as ongoing central government funding is concerned. The degree of competition between individual researchers, within the same university social work department, and between research centres (the purpose of which is not always clear) can be intense, especially with the RAE increasingly becoming the driving force behind research.

Increased competition

There has always been competition between universities for status and funds, and prior to the emergence of the 'new universities' the competition was not only between universities at the regional level but between the ivy league universities and the rest. Undoubtedly there continues to be such competition, and a measure of competition, properly framed, and played on a level playing field, is normally perceived as a 'good thing'. However, as a direct result of the RAE of 1996 and 2001 (as we are promised), for a university with research goals the stakes are very high indeed. Thus in the tough new funding climate the emergence of the 'new university' sector, as another player, further complicates and compounds the situation. In some universities for the 1996 RAE and in the lead up to that of 2001, groups of researchers have begun to resemble football teams in the Premier League. There are high transfer fees and professorial titles for 'stars', and early retirement (or rather redundancy) for those who can no longer keep up with the new pace (or do not wish to). The latter are often amongst the most experienced teachers/researchers. According to one's view there continues to be two divisions in university research: a premier league of predominantly 'old' universities, and another league of predominantly 'new' universities. From this author's perspective the situation is already quite different from the 1996 situation, in that there now seems to be one big university research league, but the 2001 RAE exercise will provide the mechanism for further change, supported or informed by changes in government policy towards future funding of research in universities. It seems likely that the trend towards specialisation and selection will continue, and that this will likely favour existing stakeholders. It follows that if there is to be a further narrowing of 'approved providers' in research, then the more structural and critical approaches to social policy and social work practice, and to understanding and conducting research might not be considered so acceptable and so become further marginalised. Particular exploratory and innovative research methodologies and grounded approaches which encourage wide participation and problem definition could find themselves more 'at risk', that is at risk of not being funded. These methodologies and approaches could include user- and carer-driven research, the more qualitative research designs (especially ethnographic research), social action research, observation studies, feminist research, and research which has explicit anti-discriminatory values. An alternative political scenario for research approaches (similar, some might argue, to green or single issue and mainstream politics in the 1980s and 1990s with 'education' as one example), is that the 'mainstream' in research will define and then absorb the 'minorstream,' diluting the latter's values along the way.

If one adds to the above list of research funding types/sources/bases the fact that applications for research funds are increasingly subject to a tendering process (the Home Office rather more than the Department of Health) then one can appreciate that the characteristics of the multi-million-pound yet still underfunded social work research business are that it is highly valued, diverse, varied, multi-layered, and, increasingly, bureaucratic and institutionalised. There is also the key issue of why shouldn't funding bodies select, or continue to select, only those institutions who, in their view, produce quality research, and in effect ignore the rest ('bit players'?). In other words why not accept the view that a 'level playing field' is an impossible, undesirable, and naïve dream.

It is difficult to know the detail about funding issues concerning social work or social care research conducted by local authorities other than to record that research departments in social services department with that title hardly exist today. There is much more emphasis on research and evaluation, and it is quite normal for these functions to be found within the auspices of quality assurance units. Recently I was informed of a local authority with its continuing research and evaluation functions but, following reorganisation, having no dedicated staff to do the job! This anecdote links in with the earlier point about some universities offering to provide a range of research services for local authority social services departments. The competition for conducting research and evaluation work in local authorities, where the funding is often minimal but where competition exists, is not only between, say, a local university and the in-house local authority research provider functions, but from the independent sector. The advantage of the independent sector is that overheads are low but the main disadvantages are lack of institutional and academic back up, and perceived absence of quality control.

Let me now move on, from describing the context for, and background to, the book, and funding issues about social work research, to introducing and explaining the book's two part structure, in some detail.

Part One – The politics of undertaking research
Activities and approaches by researchers/agencies which seek to change, empower, redistribute, or use feminist or anti-discriminatory understandings can be described, and too easily dismissed, as 'political' activities. Conversely, those understandings which, for example, support the continuation of existing practice, or make a string of 'good practice' recommendations, may be less likely to be labelled 'political' and are more acceptable. It is argued here, as illustrated by some of the contributions contained in Part One of the book, that continuity, whether of existing practice or management, or both, is as political a position to hold as change, though it is not necessarily presented as such. Neither does this mean (as could easily be construed) that the former is therefore intrinsically 'conservative' and that change is 'radical'. Yet to collect and produce new research data which can subsequently appear in a report can give the information holder a limited power to shape and distribute that information for a particular purpose or purposes, with the report carrying a stamp of authenticity, and scientific credibility, and, if conducted by a university, additional academic credibility. Agencies are usually well aware of the potential contribution research might make, and gatekeeping mechanisms, subtle and not so subtle, abound to keep a check on the research.

In Part One, then, the mechanism of 'gatekeepers' is one mechanism identified by the contributors, and commonly used by agencies (another is inertia) to gatekeep the following: knowledge (Hayes and Humphries), researchers (Harris and Paylor, and Chahal), definitions, and understandings, of ethnic minorities (Chahal), and the terms in which issues are defined and addressed (Ruegger, and McGee). It is important to acknowledge here that these issues are being addressed from researchers' perspectives. By putting oneself in the position of the social work agencies concerned one would have a different perspective, and one which then becomes more understandable, from their point of view. Yet whilst recognising these difficulties and frustrations, from a researcher's perspective, there is also an argument about not being too precious about research, to 'get real', and not be too prescriptive or defensive. For example, how would a researcher feel if an agency came along and recommended changes to a proposed piece of research which involved the research commissioner totally redefining the topic, involving all 'their' people, and having all the power? Again we come down to issues about the role and status of researchers, and agencies, and seeking to discover the 'real' purpose of the research being conducted, and ultimately, critical ethical issues about what is knowledge, how is it defined and by whom? It is both ethical and practical issues which are addressed in Part One, by researchers who have undertaken research and write with some authority on the subject.

Hayes and Humphries's chapter records experiences of conducting sensitive research into a contentious topic, namely that of immigration policy and control, and the role of health workers in such a system. The writers' argue that research topics are 'political' in the sense that research proposals are subject to a series of 'gatekeeper checks' (including those undertaken by funders and partners) and that these tend to have an investment in a conservative [and political] research agenda, than an agenda which is perceived as radical or challenging of accepted norms and values. The chapter also points to the aspirations and limits of value-driven research in seeking to bring about a measure of increased social awareness and possibly social change about sensitive political issues.

Harris and Paylor's chapter provides a challenge to perceived accepted beliefs that in order to conduct research in an appropriate and sensitive way researchers need to be similar to respondents (described by them as 'essentialism'), whether in terms of gender, disability, or other criteria. The chapter focuses on the complexity of issues, including that of 'researcher exclusion', when involved in researching those dissimilar from the self or researcher. They discuss and challenge 'essentialism', and especially its assumption that participants in the research process must conform to certain criteria shared with their co-participants. They argue that it is becoming increasingly difficult to conduct research which transgresses the boundaries set by essentialists and that no amount of research training and experience can compensate for a lack of epistemological privilege.

McGee's paper discusses the many issues concerning the negotiation of access to research participants. It presents the pros and cons of different types of negotiating access for research and the chapter contains many practical tips which have been thoughtfully considered and analysed. It is suggested, that in addition to the formal gatekeepers to the research, the 'real' gatekeepers are the research participants. McGee also discusses in some detail agencies being 'protective', which also raises questions about who is protecting whom, and why.

Chahal's chapter provides a closely argued critique of many of the assumptions made about research conducted about ethnic minority communities. It explores the vocabulary that punctuates research and language to describe or explain the black and minority ethnic population. He critically examines the use of the term 'ethnicity' and especially about definition and application in the social sciences and social research where ethnic minority groups, whether originating from Asia or Africa, are often described as constituting one group, and not groups of different individuals, identities, and cultures. He also describes his experiences as a researcher, observing that many white researchers work on black issues but that no black researchers work on non-black issues. He examines the assumptions that underpin such experiences and concludes that although there has been much research about minority ethnic communities, the way the research is conducted often contributes to 'minority ethnic communities becoming problematised' and relevant research becoming 'problem led'. The chapter concludes with a call for the social sciences to radically reassess the status of 'ethnic studies' as a separate area of study.

The first part of the book concludes with Ruegger's chapter taking forward these access and gatekeeping issues, especially the latter as they apply to access to children. In addition it explores recent shifts in policy and ideas concerning the status and rights of children to be consulted, particularly in relation to their inclusion in research where the aim is to acquire knowledge about children. Ruegger explores potential barriers erected to prevent access by agencies to direct research with children, as well as ways for researchers to understand and counter them. This is also done through a more theoretical examination of protectionist and liberationist approaches towards children, here as it relates to her research on children's perceptions of the *guardian ad litem* service.

Part Two – Research contexts, concepts and contracts
Part Two of the book is both thematic and practical, like research itself. It examines the university context within which most social work research is conducted and, together with a critique of particular methods, suggests that more-selective, filtered, vocational, and prescriptive understandings of research are emerging, with the consequences on social work practice and knowledge such changes will inevitably bring about. The main issues discussed within each chapter are essentially about *knowledge* (how is it

created? to what ends? what sort of knowledge? whose knowledge is it?) and about *power* (to produce knowledge, to include and exclude certain sorts of knowledge, to obtain research funds, power struggles between agencies and researchers) and the relation between the two. The second part is also both about researchers' experiences of practical and ethical problems connected with the knowledge they have produced and 'tactics for survival' for researchers and practitioner researchers alike. Thus it describes practical research, and discusses the politics of conducting empirical research from the perspective of the researcher. Each chapter emphasises particular issues and presents them both in terms of problems that were faced *and* the solutions that were or could be provided. Together their reflections address critical professional, ethical, and practical matters as they relate to research.

Fisher's chapter examines the way social work research is conducted in universities, and the distorting effect, impact, and costs of the Research Assessment Exercises (RAE). The chapter questions the underlying principle of selectivity as it applies to social work research conducted in universities. Fisher also examines another, and related, important issue, namely that of the nature of social work knowledge, and makes comparisons with the related areas of social policy, health subjects, and sociology. Fisher's analysis of the 1996 RAE raises key questions about the future funding arrangements of social work research conducted in universities, especially questions about the damage to social work and social work research that follows from having the selectivity principle, leading to an ever smaller crop of research centres, as the sole principle for distributing research funds.

Shaw's chapter voices the concerns of many readers of this book, and others in the field, namely that despite the importance of the rich contributions of qualitative methodologies and understandings in social work research, qualitative methodologies risk being relegated to the sidelines in key policy debates, especially about evaluation. He notes the growth of interest, in the 1990s, of evidence-based practice (or is this growth also a myth?) and supporting infrastructures for the same. His chapter presents and examines various myths connected to social work research and selects three for more-detailed examination: qualitative versus quantitative, feminist versus mainstream, and emancipatory versus mainstream.

In Harrison's chapter a social action approach to understanding and conducting research is presented, together with several illustrative case studies. The chapter outlines the aspirations and frustrations of an approach to research which seeks to give users an influential voice. Examples are included where black and minority ethnic community members were the active researchers and the research institutions operated in a supporting way. Harrison concludes by arguing that the social relations in research production can only begin to be established by conducting research from the 'bottom up', and by producing tangible change for participating communities.

Truman looks at how research findings, especially but not exclusively, drawn from quantitative research can and are misused, misappropriated, and reappropriated. In the case quoted, the research project (a survey to identify childcare nursery needs) was 'repackaged' and reused as a basis for income generation and privatisation of nursery provision. Her chapter begs the important question about knowledge generated from research, namely 'who does the knowledge belong to?' Ultimately this is a broader question about differential power relations. The chapter also includes an account of a more participatory research project which sought to address these power differentials, and was not a 'one off' or static piece of research, but been reproduced in different ways for different audiences and constituencies.

Brown and Loveridge's chapter draws on collaborative work between universities departments and social services departments, and published data from the *Social Services Research* publications (University of Birmingham) to analyse the politics of joint agency research and identify wider trends in social work research since 1991. The actual and potential tensions produced in research with collaborating partners (here the university and the social services department) in terms of research outputs (for RAE or the agency?) are articulated and specified. The chapter is based on practitioner/researchers experiences, and as well as providing a succinct overview of practitioner-collaborative research contains many tips for researchers about collaborative research.

The book's concluding chapter, by Gorman, draws on her wide range of experiences of being a tutor on a MSc in Collaborative Community Care course where agency staff undertake a research project as part of that degree's studies. The chapter highlights the many personal and political dilemmas involved in being a practitioner researcher and explores why such research, often drawing on qualitative methodologies and practitioners' understandings, can be undervalued. The chapter contains summarised testaments of practitioner researchers and highlights the importance of understanding the stages and interactions involved in research seen within the broader community care context.

Conclusion

This chapter outlined the book's structure, aims, and key themes, and problems brought about, it is argued, by an increasingly political climate and context.

The chapter also sought to argue, through exemplars, that despite the difficult climate in which to conduct research in social work and social care, quality research in this field is not only possible but remains an exciting voyage of discovery and is 'alive and kicking'. The research illustrated here reveals a breadth and depth of critical thinking about key ethical issues which can so easily be forgotten as the next research report or article deadline approaches, and the next project beckons. Yet it is almost an intrinsic element of empirical social work research and evaluation that it is essentially a pragmatic activity, constantly being negotiated and renegotiated in the light of experience and expedience. The adoption of fixed positions, for example about methodologies, can easily provoke an intransigent response. Yet on the other hand to become more flexible, and compromising, for the sake of it and to 'get on' with the project concerned, may be to yield one's strongly felt and hard-fought principles and beliefs. To some, research should be informed by methodological pluralism and ethical and political considerations, but not necessarily driven by them. Others will have another balance to strike.

In my experiences as a researcher and research director ethical issues are always present. For an individual researcher it is better to assume that research waters contain a mix of danger signs, sharks, small friendly craft, and occasional floats. These assumptions suggest that if researchers are going to enter research waters then it is advisable to choose their swimming partner and waters carefully, and that it is most important to swim under instruction, and always assume there are undercurrents. Regular swimming also hardens the skin. As outlined above, therefore, and as will be demonstrated in the following chapters in some considerable detail, research and evaluation always take place within some sort of political framework in which there are tensions between various stakeholders. With the research stakes higher, and more fully articulated than hitherto, those intrinsic tensions are considerably higher than has previously been the case. Part of the art of research, whether conducting it or managing it, is to develop a research nous, and become more aware of these political dimensions and all their multifarious aspects. This book's contributions have been selected to present a range of arguments and informed views about the politics of research, and to provide readers with both cautionary tales and practice tips in order to be more fully aware, and deal with at least some, of the political dimensions involved in social work research and evaluation. If, as I suspect, there is more of an emphasis in this book on social work research and universities, rather than practitioner research in or with agencies, then this is a reflection, in my view, of where the main larger-scale social work research and evaluation activities are increasingly concentrated and published. Nevertheless the book's contributions are relevant to all research and evaluation activities and settings.

References

Broad, B. and Fletcher, C. eds. (1993) Practitioner Social Work Research in Action, London: Whiting and Birch

Broad, B. and Saunders, L. (1998) 'Involving young people leaving care as peer researchers in a health research project: a learning experience', *Research, Policy and Planning*, 16 (1) 1-19.

Harrison, C. and Humphries, C. (1997) Putting the Praxis back into Practice, London: CCETSW

Social Work Research Association(1996), *The politics of social work research and evaluation* SWRA Leicester conference promotional literature.

Part One

The politics of undertaking research

Chapter 2
Negotiating contentious research topics

Debra Hayes and Beth Humphries

Introduction

This chapter reflects on our experiences of collaborative research between a university department and a voluntary organisation on a topic which is universally agreed to be contentious: that of immigration policy and control. For over six years the university and the agency, The Immigration Aid Unit in Manchester, have been working together on a number of projects related to immigration control, including conferences and campaigns around black prisoners and deportation (GMIAU 1992)[1]; children, families and immigration control (GMIAU 1995)[2]; immigration control and health (Cohen *et al.* 1997[3]; GMIAU 1997)[4] and the history and politics of immigration control and health (Hayes 1995). This partnership has been extremely fruitful, but tensions have arisen on a number of levels – the differing agendas of universities, the agency, and other organisations; the management, accountability and resourcing of joint projects; the push towards 'credible' research which demands that it is 'value free' and not politically committed with the associated problems of obtaining funding for such research; and lastly, the risks entailed in disseminating findings which challenge powerful groups with vested interests.

We shall explore some of these dimensions as a way of offering our reflections on the process and of clarifying the issues for ourselves. Throughout the chapter we will use the Health and Immigration Control project we have most recently collaborated on as a case study to illustrate the themes raised above.

What makes research contentious?

Sensitive research has been described as exploring 'areas of social life that are contentious or highly conflictual' because 'in such situations research can be seen by those involved as threatening the alignments, interests or security of those in a conflict, especially those who are in positions of relative power' (Renzetti & Lee 1993 p.6). Our research into health and immigration could be said to fit these criteria, for a number of reasons. First, immigration has become a significant political issue on all sides of the political spectrum; second, it has become a key arena for the maintenance of racist ideas albeit often in coded language; and third, it is a mechanism by which, 'Now, across Europe . . . far-Right ideas are being incorporated into mainstream political debate and practice' (Bentley 1995, p.57).

This is, then, inherently a political and highly charged arena. In addition the consensus around immigration has shifted to the point where challenges to the order of things are strictly limited to tinkering at the edges to somehow make immigration control fairer:

> *'Labour could break away from the absurd position that good race relations depend on racist immigration policies and draft a rational non-racist immigration policy'* (Guardian 11 February 1997 p.15).

The assumption here is that immigration controls are necessary, and that it is possible to construct controls that do not affect some groups more than others. To take a position of opposition to *all* immigration control then is considered ludicrous and outside the parameters of acceptable ideas. Yet, this is precisely the position adopted by this research team, because immigration control is illogical and irrational and inherently discriminatory. At the heart of control will always be the issue of who is deserving of entry and who is not, who is likely to be socially costly and who is not. It is by its nature rooted in ideas of nation and empire – that *we* simply cannot afford to cope with all of *them*. On the question of numbers alone it is irrational, and sustains a mythology about hordes of needy immigrants trying to get access to *our* country and resources. The statistics show that more people leave the UK annually than enter; for example in 1993 213,000 people came into the UK and 216,000 left (Office for National Statistics 1997, figure 2.6, p.16). However, arguments around arithmetic are problematic and feed into the idea that unemployment, poverty, homelessness, and a whole range of other social ills would be less evident if the population was smaller. Since its inception, immigration control has targeted particular groups considered to be problematic, from Jewish refugees fleeing persecution in the nineteenth century to black immigrants in the twentieth (Hayes 1995). Any suggestion that it could be non-racist fails to appreciate its role in problematising outsiders and propping up the ideology of racism.

Such racism extends beyond a country's frontiers, and touches the lives of all those citizens perceived to be 'outsiders', resulting in their internal policing by state organisations. Liz Fekete describes this shift across Europe to a 'welfare sneak system' where state officials participate in policing immigration:

> *'This then is the shape of welfare to come. For the conditions attached to benefits shift the concept of welfare . . . from concern to coercion, from rights to duties. And this in turn shifts the balance in the state apparatus from welfare to authoritarianism'* (Fekete 1997 p.16)

It will be clear then that such a position leads to research which is highly critical of government policy, is explicitly political in its values and aims, and hopes to challenge the interests of powerful groups.

Welfare and immigration

This interest in the ever-increasing role of welfare agencies in the internal workings of immigration control has been an important dimension in our work. Not only is eligibility for a significant number of benefits and social entitlements now linked to immigration status, but agencies of welfare provision from the DSS (Department of Social Security) to the NHS (National Health Service) have a formal and ever-closer relationship with the IND (Immigration and Nationality Department), providing it with invaluable information on immigration status. It is these agencies which maintain and sustain ideas around just who is deserving of welfare and which have machinery in place to gatekeep resources. The massive implications of this for black residents are a key feature of our research. For those managing these tensions any research exposing these issues may be seen as threatening and contentious. We wish to bring to the attention of the health service, welfare, and probation workers the process by which they are being routinely incorporated into state surveillance of their patients/clients. There is a risk that social work values such as anti-discrimination have become so individualistic as to miss completely the implications of the daily working relationship between the 'caring' agencies of the state and the Home Office (Cohen 1996).

Taking risks

The scope for misuse was a concern for us in exploring the operation of internal immigration controls within the NHS. We conducted a distinct piece of research on the operation of the NHS (Charges to Overseas Visitors) Regulation, (see Cohen *et al.*, 1997) within both hospitals and GP surgeries. We suspected the regulations were being applied in an *ad hoc* manner and possibly even in a racist one. We worried that any exposure of inconsistency might result in a tightening up of procedures, which could adversely affect black users of the NHS, an already disadvantaged group in terms of access to health care (Torkington, 1991; Ahmad, 1993).

> *'The task of recognising and resolving ethical and political problems is made difficult, and at times impossible, because other parties have motives and perceptions quite different than those of the researcher'*
> (J. E. Sieber in Renzetti and Lee 1993 p.14).

These concerns were further compounded by our knowledge that the history of research in the field of race and health does not make comfortable reading (Ahmad, 1993). It has problematised 'race', focused on 'cultural difference' and contributed to 'making black people sick'. Torkington concludes:

> *'It becomes obvious from reading through some of the many volumes in the field of health that race relations research in the past avoided looking at institutional racism and concentrated instead on cultural and biological factors in explaining what are clearly the effects of racism and class oppression'* (Torkington 1994, p.40).

This knowledge, however, was to clarify our need to produce research which focused on *racism* itself in the experience of health care, and vindicated our desire to look at the structures at work in the NHS, which affect black users of the service.

An understanding of the political climate helped to galvanise our resolve in the need to go ahead. In short, the progression towards increasing internal immigration control is moving apace in any case, with disastrous consequences for black people. They are already being asked to prove their residence status and consequently their rights to entitlement in many welfare arenas, including the NHS. We already knew there had been inappropriate refusals of free treatment at some London hospitals, with one hospital in particular being reported to the Commission for Racial Equality regarding allegations of over-zealous screening of Kurdish refugees, that is, asking for proof of eligibility before offering treatment (Guardian 21 February 1995). In addition the government of the day made it clear it wanted closer links between the NHS and the IND, and a tightening up of procedures in this field, as it had done successfully in other fields like the welfare benefits and criminal justice systems. Staff in the NHS are being pushed to

> *'find better ways of controlling access to free medical treatment . . . and to improve procedures to enable providers of benefits and services to identify ineligible persons from abroad'.*
> (Home Secretary, Michael Howard, Press Release 13 October 1993).

There have been no signs that the New Labour government are prepared to take a different approach to immigration policy, and we must assume a continuation of previous government policies.

We have, therefore, moved ahead in the knowledge that the only acceptable framework is one which 'fronts up' the anti-racist agenda, and openly seeks to challenge the racist consequences of internal immigration control. We have also offered training to workers in the NHS on these issues in the hope that by highlighting these realities about their role we can begin to provide a focus for resistance.

Legitimacy in research

Despite debates about objectivity and value freedom in research in the social sciences, it remains a contested area. We share the view that 'it is difficult to see how societal and individual values might actually be absent from the research process' (Williams & May 1996 p.132). Indeed we did not wish to proclaim a value-free stance, but rather to question both the possibility and the desirability of value freedom in research, because 'neutrality is not enough, for neutrality is culturally and historically specific' (Ahmad 1993 p.17). Nevertheless, within academic institutions it can still be difficult to achieve respectability when research is viewed as 'political', because a hegemony of neutral research still dominates the social science research community (Hammersley 1995). Consequently some of those who venture into the real world of politics or policy formulation find that their 'academic prowess is questioned by their more traditional colleagues or that they themselves face personal dilemmas of value free or value committed research' (Torkingon 1991 p.39).

Liz Stanley characterises 'the academic mode of production' as having a partic-ular set of politics and ideology as part of the conditions of its existence. These politics centre on scientism, 'that is on essentially Cartesian ideas about "science", "knowledge", "the research process", "theory", and "expertise" ' (Stanley 1990 pp.4-5). Within the academic mode there are those who act as official and unofficial gatekeepers of academic inputs and outputs. Scrutiny of research proposals at university and funding council levels are likely to be influenced by these perceptions of what 'proper research' looks like, and about who can be a 'knower' and what can be known. Scientific knowledge has been privileged over other forms of knowledge, its dominance predicated upon the authority of a research community concerned about the truth to claims of knowledge (see Humphries 1997). From this community has come a set of rules and ideas about the construction of knowledge which have been the orthodoxy in social research. This results in the 'exclusion of other forms of knowledge and a denial of their legitimacy' (Edwards & Usher 1994 p.158).

Writers such as Hammersley exercise this exclusion by declaring feminist, critical and anti-racist truths as outside the norms of legitimate research. He believes research should not be value committed or political, but that 'it should be directed at no other immediate goal than the production of knowledge' (Hammersley 1995 p.118). The point here is that this view represents a vision of legitimate research still dominant in universities and funding organisations. Research proposals which have an explicit political commitment, based on a notion of 'praxis', or which claim to be 'emancipatory' are likely to face problems with those gatekeepers. The problem is that although value freedom is not a feasible goal, those commissioning or funding research assume an attitude of 'objectivity', not recognising their position is value loaded because it is often based on normative views of society. As a result, research proposals such as ours are required to highlight some aspects of their aims and methods more than others.

Further barriers
Universities operate in a climate of intense competition, and some are in serious debt. Their government funding increasingly depends on the profile of their staff in relation to publication, consultancies, and research grants. They are traditionally conservative in stepping onto new research ground where there are risks. The new universities especially have much to prove about their academic credibility. Some universities scrutinise research proposals submitted in their name, at every level from head of department to vice-chancellor. Proposals have to run the gauntlet not only of university priorities but of personal prejudice, degrees of caution, and vested interests. Universities are not independent of the State or of powerful interests in society. Some understanding of these dynamics is crucial for those steering proposals through these systems.

On the other hand, the rush for a high research profile can work to the advantage of contentious research. In a climate where staff's research interests are being encouraged, and where they are seen to be competent in delivering outcomes, the substantive topic may not be the most important criterion for receiving university support. It is these contradictory forces which have to be negotiated and managed. In our research we were able to manoeuvre within these interests, so that a research topic and approach which at a different time may not have been seen to be acceptable found approval because they promised a distinctive niche in which several staff had shown an active interest.

Similar processes operate at the level of funding bodies. It is difficult to discern the informal criteria by which they make decisions about grant allocation. It is likely that a track record, personal contacts, and prejudices all play a part. In the case of contentious research, a design which is pitched in ways which do not appear directly political may stand a better chance. This is because, although funding bodies may have an explicit interest in certain topics, as we discussed above, these interests are not value free. However, funders may hold a traditional view of research, and *purport* to value freedom and neutrality. Applicants may have to guess what those values are, perhaps 'foregrounding' non-contentious and 'safe' elements of their proposals. Our study which aimed to identify the ways health professionals are involved in policing immigration status and gatekeeping resources, accordingly was successful because it emphasised its aim to develop a code of ethics for health workers on their changing role, and also because we offered training to those health workers on the issues it raised for them on both practical and ethical levels. Such training was designed not only to acquaint health services workers with immigration legislation and policy, but to raise questions about the legitimacy of the role within policies which have been designed for them and other health and welfare workers. We should not be naïve about the relationship of the major funding bodies and the universities to national economic goals and business interests, and the influence these have on how research moneys are to be spent, regardless of the language in which criteria for proposals are framed.

Managing collaborative research – some practical problems
Working in partnership with communities and community-based organisations is an important principle for some university-based researchers. It is a way of ensuring research is realistic and relevant to need, and it fulfils the (now forgotten?) aim of old polytechnics to serve the local community. Such partnerships are also approved by government and indeed may be a requirement for research funding. However the practicalities of working together in managing joint funding have seldom been explored, especially where the subject matter is sensitive, and we offer some reflections on our experience of collaborative work. Our joint project on immigration control and health was funded partly by a grant-giving charity, with matching funding (in kind) given by the university, the result of which was a distinct research element on the charging of overseas visitors within the NHS. Other aims of the project were the provision of direct training and the production of training materials to health professionals. A steering committee was set up to manage the project.

Much of the tension which emerged arose from the different agendas of the voluntary organisation and the university. The voluntary organisation is engaged in offering free immigration advice and most of the staff are working flat out on casework, or organising high profile anti-deportation campaigns, as well as the demoralising task of searching for further funding to ensure survival in each successive year. Understandably research is not seen as a priority, and there are misconceptions about the nature of work within universities. Further, the organisation is funded by local authorities who expect a casework service to people in their areas having immigration problems, and needs to ensure that that service is delivered appropriately, and that resources are not diverted into other work. The financial insecurity of the organisation and its workers led to anxieties about the involvement of their colleagues in the project, and perhaps sensitivity about possible outcomes which might have implications for the role played by local authorities in internal controls. The 'hand that fed them' might be severely bitten.

The university prioritised the research, but did not necessarily prioritise the training component within the NHS. The research workers were pulled by these two agendas and were often drawn into organising conferences, contributing to developing training materials and other work not related to their remit. The workers were located within the agency and the university making them isolated, dislocated from each other and also the other workers engaged in the more routine tasks at each workplace. These problems raise issues about accountability. Assumptions had been made about how supervision and support would take place within the two organisations with different line management structures; unfortunately this lack of attention to detail in practice caused confusion and uncertainty. These problems are of course not unique to contentious research, but in a climate where organisations feel under siege, where future funding for both voluntary agencies and universities is uncertain, the nature of the content and values 'foregrounded' in controversial activities can be seen as rather tempting providence.

A further dimension involved the registration for PhD studies as part of the project. The fact that this is an expectation at all is, of course, indicative of current demands within higher education and went hand in hand with the partial funding of the project. What was to prove problematic in choosing a PhD supervisor was this question of politics and values, since the power dynamic makes it difficult for a student to ask potential supervisors questions about these issues. The supervisory relationship is not, of course, an equal one and the assumption at any introductory meetings is that it is the potential supervisor who is vetting the student and not the other way around. Certainly published work can give an insight into the values and interests of possible supervisors and hopefully networking in the particular field of interest can open up options. Nevertheless, a student remains less powerful in this process, and certainly in this project it took some time to locate someone with the academic background as well as the interests and politics in the subject matter.

Research and action
So, in what sense then does any of this matter? As stated earlier there is considerable evidence in the failure of much of the 'race' and health research, most specifically in terms of its inability to be translated into committed action. From rickets to TB, through schizophrenia to HIV/AIDS, research has focused on and exaggerated perceived racial/cultural difference, and has not placed racism at the heart of black people's experience of health, disease, and health care.

The priority for us, then, was to look at practical strategies in the health arena which take account of the centrality of racism and offer a challenge to it:

> '*Inevitably, this must go beyond the study of racism in one institution – the NHS – to examine the importance of structural inequalities and the existence of a pervasive racism within the welfare state in a society in which black people have been defined ideologically as a "problem" or a "threat"*'. (Stubbs in Ahmad, 1993 p.41).

Running parallel to the piece of research on charging, we offered training within the NHS to workers concerned about the implications of immigration control. Clearly this was advertised and delivered in a way consistent with the values and politics expressed here. This was not an 'add on' at the end of the research to assist in dissemination, but an integral part of the project. We also held a national conference, the first of its kind for health workers to explore these issues. It was clear from the numbers attracted (over a hundred delegates from across the whole country and from a wide variety of health care settings) and the tone of the conference that it had struck a chord with many, who had perhaps not previously had a venue to express their concerns and question practice within the NHS. In these ways we attempted a praxis which linked research closely to action for change.

It is difficult to see how some of this work could have been done without the clear political framework created within the project. Without that the potential would have been for this piece of research, like so many others, to make black people the object without making any real difference to their experience of health care. However, what we found from the conference and from the requests for training, was that the mainstream NHS services were not well represented. It was the specialist services for particular ethnic groups, the HIV services, agencies dealing with the health and welfare of refugees, and agencies concerned with challenging racism, who engaged with the issues. The real question here is not that managers within the NHS would openly subvert this work, but in the current political climate they just would not see the question of their role in immigration control as a training priority. Contentiousness in this sense, then, may be anything outside that perceived to be essential in a budget-led NHS. Power within welfare institutions can be exercised simply by rendering invisible the concerns of the oppressed. Their concerns are real for, however marginal these issues may seem in the complex and changing arena of health care delivery, each time a black person enters a hospital or visits a health centre, form filling and questioning about ethnic origin now have sinister overtones, irrespective of their immigration status.

In the long term it would be over optimistic to expect a piece of research on the charging of overseas visitors within the NHS to halt the stampede towards increasingly restrictive immigration control, particularly the move towards internal policing of immigration through welfare. Nevertheless, providing an alternative voice is crucial. Despite our difficulties in attracting the interest of the mainstream within the NHS, we have now a network of individuals across the country who wish to challenge the operation of internal controls and who are using materials and resources produced by the project to raise the profile of this problem. Many of these people work within specialist teams within the NHS or are responsible for health care delivery in the community. It is crucial for those workers in the NHS, black and white, concerned about their new roles and responsibilities in relation to immigration control, that there is this alternative voice. There is evidence of dissatisfaction. For example, the General Secretary of the National Union of Civil and Public Servants within the NHS has said, 'Such measures will cause misery and distress to millions of British citizens and damage the standing of hundreds and thousands of health and social services staff' (Guardian 20 July 1995).

Contentious research can perhaps provide a focus for such dissatisfaction, when those working at the front line may be in a too vulnerable a situation to offer such a challenge. If the practice within hospitals can be changed at the point of accessing health care, this could have positive consequences for those black people currently forced to account for their right to welfare when they are sick. We hope that one outcome will be an ongoing forum amongst all of these interests, towards development of strategies to make the alternative voice heard.

Conclusion

We have raised a number of issues about the politics of contentious research, especially where colleagues attempt to collaborate across organisations. These concerns are underpinned by a recognition that a commitment to anti-racism is limited if it does not recognise discourses about 'race' and disease which not only legitimise the exclusion of black people, in particular, from the UK, but which make all 'outsiders within' infectious, unacceptable, and dangerous, and liable to account for their eligibility for health and welfare services in ways not required of other people.

Within this framework, we have explored macro issues related to bureaucratic processes, applying for research moneys and credibility of political research in a wider research community. We have highlighted more micro issues about the management of collaborative research, the tensions among different organisational agendas, and aspects raised for the academic interests of individuals.

In terms of disseminating contentious research findings, perhaps it is unrealistic to expect a welcome from mainstream services for which our findings are not a priority. The conference however, served among other things to identify a network of groups and individuals who perhaps represent the best hope of bringing pressure for change. Local authority and health service trade unions, concerned about the ways in which their members' jobs are being redfined, have shown themselves willing to engage with our work.

This last point brings us back to one of our fundamental concerns, the role expected of health and welfare professionals in internal controls, a role far beyond the imaginings of people entering the professions. More seriously, it is a role to which their training does not alert them in terms of the ethical implications of being obliged to pass on to central government departments, information not directly relevant to a request for help or treatment. Bur what kind of training is appropriate? The tension in training is between helping professionals to be more competent oppressors, more efficient detectors of 'illegality', and being more attuned to the inherent racist nature of the immigration policy. A risk of dissemination of findings of contentious research is that it may alert policy makers to the gaps and contradicitions in legislation and policy statements, only to close them against those perceived to be alien. A key contentious but necessary element of our research is to bring to the attention of practitioners and educators this dimension of growing surveillance function of social work and health professionals, and the need for training which both subverts and challenges oppressive practices. Bringing this out into the open and calling for an examination of the implications of the surveillance role seems to us to be an appropriate role for social work. A unity of thought and action (praxis), a way of being which does not separate 'research' from struggles for social transformation, is at the heart of contentious research.

References

Ahmad, W. I. (ed.) (1993) *'Race' and health in contemporary Britain.* Buckingham, Open University Press.

Bentley, S. (1995) 'Merrick and the British campaign to stop immigration: populist racism and political influence', Race and Class 36 (3).

Cohen, S. (1996) 'Anti-semitism, immigration controls and the welfare state' in D. Taylor (ed) *Critical Social Policy: a Reader*, London, Sage, 27-47.

Cohen, S., Hayes, D., Humphries, B., Sime, C. (1997) *Immigration Controls and Health: Implementation of The NHS (Charges to Overseas Visitors) Regulations. A survey of NHS Trusts and General Practices in Greater Manchester and Inner London*, Manchester Metropolitan University.

Edwards, R., & Usher, R,, (1994) *Postmodernism and Education*, London and New York, Routledge.

Fekete, L. 1997 'Blackening the economy: the path to convergence', *Race and Class*, 39(1), 1-18.

GMIAU 1992 *Campaign Against Double Punishment Resource Pack*. Manchester: GMIAU.

GMIAU 1995 *Children, the Family and Immigration Control Resource Pack*. Manchester: GMIAU.

GMIAU 1997 *Health and Immigration Control Resource Pack*. Manchester: GMIAU.

Hammersley, M. (1995) *The Politics of Social Research*, Sage.

Hayes, D. (1995) *Race, Health and Immigration Control*, MMU working paper, Manchester, Manchester Metropolitan University.

Humphries, B. (1997) 'From critical thought to emancipatory action: contradictory research goals?' *Sociological Research Online*, 2(1), <http://www.socresonline.org.uk/socresonline/2/2/8.html>

Office for National Statistics 1997 *Annual Abstract of Statistics*, no.133, London Stationary Office.

Renzetti, C. M. & Lee, R. M., (eds), 1993 *Researching Sensitive Topics*, London, Sage.

Stanley, L. (1990) 'Feminist praxis and the academic mode of production: an editorial introduction' in Stanley, L. (ed.) *Feminist Praxis*, London and New York, Routledge, 3-19.

Torkington, N. P. K. (1991) *Black Health – a Political Issue*, Liverpool, Catholic Association for Racial Justice/Liverpool IHE.

Williams, M. & May, T. (1996) *Introduction to the Philosophy of Social Research*, UCL Press Ltd.

Notes

1,2 All the Resource Packs are available from Greater Manchester Immigration Aid Unit, 400
& 4 Cheetham Hill Road, Manchester M8 9LE, price per pack.

3. Available from Department of Applied Community Studies, Manchester Metropolitan University, 799 Wilmslow Road, Didsbury, Manchester M20 2PP, price £5 per copy.

Chapter 3
The politics of difference:
researching those dissimilar from the self

Jennifer Harris and Ian Paylor

Introduction

This focus of this chapter is the thorny problem of being different to those one researches in a prevailing research climate which emphasises the imperative of being the same. Such discourses permeate the methodologies of feminism and disability research to name only two and their proponents are open to allegations of essentialism[1]. In the chapter, we address how we managed in conducting research 'against the political tide of opinion'. We undertook very different studies Jennifer Harris encountered problems with essentialism in a study of Deaf[2] people, whilst Ian Paylor had similar experiences in studying women prisoners. whilst the practical solutions to these problems differed, the underlying politics contributing to them were the same. We discuss how 'different' we are to the groups studied, why this mattered, how essentialism manifested itself and what we did about it. Finally we ask, are there real benefits to being 'different' that are being neglected by the concentration within these methodologies on sameness?

Essentialism and Epistemological Privilege

The notion of essentialism comprises the charge that participants in the research process must conform to certain criteria shared with their co-participants. Below we produce evidence that in post-modern Britain it is becoming increasingly difficult to conduct research which transgresses the boundaries set by essentialists. Briefly, essentialism dictates that to be the *same*, to hold epistemological privilege, confers the right to be held as authentic and 'expert' in a given field. Conversely, no amount of research training and experience can compensate for a lack of epistemological privilege; being *'different'* places researchers on the margins and denies rights to participation.

In relation to social work, Fuller and Petch (1995), whilst not condemning out of hand 'external' researchers, question their ability to fully understand social work or the social work process. In an otherwise excellent book on research methods, Fuller and Petch's (1995) overall objective is to make the case for social workers to be more actively engaged in research. Social work practitioners, Fuller and Petch (1995) argue, have certain advantages as researchers; they have a 'research agenda rooted in knowledge of practice'; they 'possess complementary problem analysis and desegregation skills'; they are expert interviewers and recorders of data and they have superior knowledge of sources and access to data.

> *'Practitioners enjoy advantages over external researchers, who are inevitably at a remove from the front line and commonly need intensive discussions with practitioners to confirm or refine definitions of what is important or what makes sense'* (Fuller and Petch 1995: 9).

Social work practitioners undertaking research, Fuller and Petch (1995) argue, are much better placed than external researchers to develop a 'participative style' of engagement; they display an 'extra level of commitment to its success-ful completion' and the project is more likely to reach a wider audience and other practitioners are more willing to act upon any findings.

This is all written in the spirit of encouraging more social work practitioners to undertake research, but, given the problems we have encountered which we discuss below, these remarks along with others in the field of nursing (Wibberley and Kenny 1994; Ryan 1993) could be construed as the first manoeuvrings in the construction of barriers in the field of social care research. Certain research topics may require certain skills (Lee 1993; Renzetti and Lee 1993) but these are not necessarily best supplied by an 'insider', especially when couched in such essentialist terms.

How did we arrive at such a situation? Whilst it is complicated to trace the origins of such ideas which exist at the level of 'common sense knowledge', there seems little doubt that the identity politics movement began in second wave feminism and really began to take root in the research community from the mid-1980s. Even whilst promulgating essentialist philosophy, feminists began to acknowledge problems of its effects. Halberg (in Hall *et al.* 1992), in an honest and open appraisal, notes this as a tension between 'objectivism' (which includes rationalists, empiricists, foundationalists, and essentialists) and 'relativism' (described as 'the dialectical antithesis of objectivism' by Halberg). These 'opposing trends' she states

'. . . alert us to some of the incompatible tendencies in feminist epistemologies. The problems may be briefly described in the following way: If existing "tradi-tional" knowledge is considered false, and not only inadequate because of its one-sidedness, there must be possibilities for a true(r) knowledge. Also, there should be plausible and tenable ways of explaining why traditional knowledge is male-biased, whilst feminist knowledge is not. If both kinds of knowledge, the "male" and the "female" (or feminist) are considered biased, we are faced with a kind of relativism entailing that different views are equally (either) true (or false). . . . Unless one supposes that male-biased theories somehow misdescribe reality and misrepresent how things are, it is difficult to make sense of much of feminist science criticism. This assumption, however, tends to lead to some kind of objectivism: but objectivism is at the same time associated with a masculine epistemology, which feminism sets out to oppose. Thus we land in the difficult situation of having to defend a kind of "feminist objectivism" whilst rejecting all other forms of objectivist claims. Consequently, feminist epistemologies need very strong and convincing arguments. They will have to answer some complicated questions about why women and/or feminists have correct versions of how things really are, and why they are the only ones who enjoy this privileged position.' (Halberg in Hall 1992; 373).

The fundamental tensions in feminist epistemology described above by Halberg are presented in depth to illuminate the rationale driving essentialism. The tautological half-Nelson in which feminists end up (as depicted by Halberg) leaves them in the position of arguing for feminist knowledge to be viewed as a 'special' case but denying that this should be 'measured' by the same objective stick as 'male-based theories'. Thus, essentialism creates problems even for its proponents. Undoubtedly this position is unresolved within the research community since our experiences appear to suggest that instead of searching for these convincing arguments which might justify a position of epistemological privilege, the notions have merely become incorporated into 'folk lore' and research procedures designed around such privilege without engaging in the 'right to know(ledge)' debate. Within feminism this right to knowledge is described by Halberg (ibid) as 'feminist standpoint epistemology':

'It is founded on the claim that women have a cognitively privileged position in society, so that their knowledge is superior to men's knowledge. This privileged position is taken to be rooted in or generated by women's experiences, defined in a broad sense.' (Halberg in Hall. 1992.373).

However, later Halberg considers the grounding of such privilege upon 'experience' as problematic – acknowledging this as an 'extremely vague term' (ibid.377):

'Experiences are always influenced by the contexts surrounding them and therefore never coherent or identical for all women . . . I reject experience as a grounding for feminist epistemologies and I oppose the proposals that men and women do have different ways to knowledge' (ibid.377).

Our own experiences of encountering essentialism demonstrate that this is an unhelpfully narrow framework within which to conduct research. Below, we detail the ways in which we have encountered essentialism in research projects. This comprises ways in which we have been challenged by participants in the field on the grounds that 'we are not the same' (as they are) and therefore we cannot experience or interpret their world in a truthful or valid way. In Harris's case, this was on the grounds that she is hearing, researching the world of Deaf people; whilst in Paylor's this was in relation to his masculinity in interviewing female prisoners.

To be clear, we do not deny that we are in fact different in these crucial respects from the populations we studied. Where we oppose essentialism is inasmuch as the latter places fundamental importance upon the *necessity* of similarity for the purposes of undertaking research. In other words, the essentialist imperative is that it is a deficit to be dissimilar from the researched population, whereas our view is that it can be advantageous. As we will demonstrate, essentialism cannot be divorced from its effects.

Being 'different' to our respondents

Essentialism has serious implications for research since it prescribes suitability of certain researchers based around notions of shared identities, whilst simultaneously creating 'outgroups' who do not conform to these criteria. The effects of essentialism are more difficult to analyse than to describe. In saying that we are 'different' to those studied, the people pointing this out aim to make a political point. In other words, we know that we are different and although we would not say that this did not matter, we did not think of it as a major obstacle in the research enterprise. Pointing it out *in this way* was done for a particular political purpose – it throws into question our ability to produce valid research because of our difference. It is therefore a very important challenge to be recognised by researchers.

Essentialism permeates the texts in many research areas. In particular, feminist literature (Oakley 1981, 1987; Smith 1987; DeVault 1990; Fishman 1990; Reinharz 1992; Collins 1993) contains the notion of 'shared sisterhood' and the assumption that men cannot successfully undertake research with women. Much more recently, essentialist ideas have begun to permeate the emerging fields of Deaf Studies and Disability Politics. In our accounts below, we describe the effects of essentialism within our own research projects.

Jennifer Harris: Encountering Essentialism in Deafness Research

Baker-Shenk and Kyle (1990.65) have claimed that only Deaf interviewers can achieve rapport in the research enterprise and that any such undertaken by hearing researchers would suffer from 'cultural conflict'. Both of the major research centres undertaking research with Deaf people (Bristol and Durham

Universities) argue vehemently that research with Deaf people can *only* be undertaken by use of a specific philosophy of research practices within which Deaf people's interaction is video-recorded. For example, Jones and Pullen (1990.9) in reference to their methods note the following:

> In order to be true to the aim of the project – *to provide a deaf perspective* – it was considered important to find a way of conducting a deaf-to-deaf interview in the indigenous sign language of each country. So that the interviews could be conducted in sign language, *they had to be video recorded*. At the same time (where possible) a simultaneous translation into the spoken language of the country was made by a sign language interpreter into a microphone (Jones and Pullen 1990.9) (my emphasis).

This statement embodies the currently prevalent working philosophy within the Deafness research community concerning the inappropriateness of hearing researchers interviewing Deaf subjects. This philosophy has two parts. Firstly, being mindful of the ways in the past in which Deaf people have been used as models of deficiency in relation to hearing people, the emphasis currently in research procedure is to capitalise upon the common feelings of fellowship amongst Deaf people by utilising Deaf interviewers and in so doing, this, it is claimed, provides an accurate 'deaf perspective'. Although the intention of these authors is to circumvent the issue of 'epistemological privilege' by providing a 'deaf perspective', this depends crucially upon whether one takes the view that this is really the case when Deaf people are used as data collectors, whilst hearing people undertake data analysis and report writing. My view, however, is that this procedure is potentially oppressive and in many respects dishonest, as the intention is to make a claim to validity based upon the similarity of the researcher and researched group. My own view on this important point is that it is better to make no claims to the research being other than it is – a hearing person's account of Deaf people's experience. I therefore took the latter route, but in so doing ran the gauntlet of opposition by the essentialists.

Secondly, bearing in mind the fact that part of the philosophy is that Deaf people form a separate culture to hearing people, it is considered by researchers (particularly at Bristol) to be 'culturally incorrect' for hearing people to attempt to interview Deaf people across the boundaries, as it were. This is based upon the view that the history of oppression by hearing people would ensure that Deaf people in an interview situation with a hearing researcher would be overawed and compliant, thus yielding the type of data that the researcher wants, but which is intrinsically flawed. This view, often propounded but seldom overtly contained in methodological literature, is promoted by researchers at Bristol University's Deaf Studies Centre (see Baker-Shenk and Kyle 1990). Data gathered by hearing researchers is therefore, in their view, flawed or, at the very least, heavily biased. This stance also rests upon assumptions concerning researchers from Universities' 'middle class culture', and hearing people's inherent superiority and paternalism towards Deaf people (ibid.66-7). These researchers also imply that participant observation will be *tainted* by hearing status:

> Our training tells us to respect these differences from our own norms. Some of us are even trained to learn and adopt the practices of other groups in order to become 'participant observers' and do good ethnographic research. But we still do this from a dominant cultural perspective and we have great difficulty in submerging our identity in the culture, (Baker-Shenk and Kyle 1990.68).

Baker-Shenk and Kyle's views on the research enterprise conducted between Deaf and hearing people are, I believe, unnecessarily pessimistic. Although their arguments are powerful and extremely influential in the field, I opposed them as guiding principles for my study for the following reasons:

First, the rigidity of his view on cultural correctness leaves aside the fact that not all Deaf people subscribe to the view that Deaf people have a separate culture to hearing people and that some have a predominant wish for integration (cf. Harris 1995).

Second, the claim of presenting the 'true deaf perspective' by employing deaf interviewers is dubious. A major assumption made in Jones and Pullen's (1990) research for example is that Deaf people from different countries in Europe would naturally identify in a major way with a Deaf interviewer. Put differently, the authors make the assumption that Deafness has a master status above that of race. Currently, there is no research evidence to support this view. This perspective also contains an assumption that Deaf people can only really share their ideas with other Deaf people and that they would be incapable of presenting them to hearing people. This seems to me to represent a gross disservice to the capabilities of Deaf people and to make *a priori* assumptions concerning their levels of interaction with hearing people and their willingness (or otherwise) to participate in their research.

These authors' obsession with 'purity' in the research process, it is asserted here, is not only extreme, it can be seen to be founded upon very dubious principles. Certainly the historical legacy of the dominance:inferiority power relation must be considered and sensitivity exercised but surely studies by hearing people can be accepted for what they are: studies by hearing researchers concerning Deaf people? (cf. Harris 1995) If all research followed this premise only men could research men, only women could research women, and only people of the same race could research each other; the vast majority of anthropological literature would be deemed useless. Furthermore, the possibilities for broadening rather than narrowing our understanding of cross-cultural difference would be greatly diminished as a direct result.

To be clear, we must as a research community acknowledge the effects of differential power relations in the research process. However, if we allow essentialism and political correctness to drive the research process, we are in danger of delimiting the fields within which we conduct research to only those individuals who have the same characteristics as ourselves. Whilst we perhaps do not always experience the same oppressions as those we seek to study, there is everything to gain and little to lose from attempting to understand the perspectives of those different to ourselves. As Barnes states:

'If disability research is about researching oppression, and I would argue that it is, then researchers should not be professing '"mythical independence" to disabled people, but joining with them in their struggles to confront and overcome this oppression. . . . There is no independent or middle ground when researching oppression; academics and researchers can only be with the oppressors or with the oppressed' (Barnes, C. 1996.110).

The point here is that researchers in these fields are being questioned, not only on their difference from those they research and their reasons for wishing to studying them, but also on their political allegiances and sympathies. Indeed, as Barnes makes clear above, the 'wrong' answer has potentially disastrous consequences for the research process.

Ian Paylor:
Encountering essentialism in research with women prisoners
Power relations are central to the essentialism debate. Feminist writers equate women's shared disadvantaged position in society with shared powerlessness. At the heart of the argument is the notion that women are better at interviewing women; that a special relationship exists between all women which cannot be replicated by male interviewers. The central theme of the feminist case is that the shared experience of sisterhood facilitates rapport, which in turn produces qualitatively superior data in an intensive interview situation. It is argued that women are more likely to open up to another woman, especially where private or sensitive material is sought. (Oakley 1981; Finch 1984). The obvious

assumption within this stance is that interview situations where men interview women, or where women interview men, will not produce data as rich as that in woman-to-woman interviews.

However, studies strongly suggest that the gender of the interviewer is not an insurmountable barrier to establishing rapport and achieving reliable results in qualitative interviewing (Williams and Heikes 1993), and my own (Paylor 1995) experience of interviewing women in Styal Prison, staff and inmates alike, was that the relationship between myself and the female interviewees was a warm, productive, and satisfactory one. Indeed, as the subject matter of the interviews concerned very personal details such as living arrangements on release, it was noticeable and surprising that the female interviewees provided far-more-detailed personal information than the male interviewees in the study. Far from gender being problematic, it seems in my study to have aided the research process.

All this does not deny that a female researcher having access to the women in my study may have developed the same depth of understanding and empathy. It does, however, contradict the feminist case which states that being a man is a hindrance when interviewing women. Carol B. Warren (1988) sees the method-ological accounts describing female fieldworkers as possessing 'greater communicative skills and less threatening nature[s]' as part of a rich gender folkloric tradition whose myths, she goes on to say, should be approached 'not as revealed truths about fieldwork relations, but as accounts – as texts in their own right, to be read as texts' (p.64).

However, closer examination of accounts by feminist writers indicates factors other than gender which operate in the interview situation. Oakley (1981), for example, was a mother herself and was therefore able to talk knowledgeably with the women respondents in her study on motherhood. Finch's account of interviews in two research projects (1984) similarly points to factors other than gender which served to facilitate rapport. Finch let it be known to the clergy wives in her study that she herself was married to a clergyman at the time. Thus her respondents were able to see her as 'one of them'. However, the women respondents in Finch's playgroup study wanted to be able to place her in terms of 'marriage and motherhood' and Finch shared neither of these statuses at that time. Finch noted that there was 'some unease in the interview' in consequence (Finch 1984. p78). It appears therefore that shared gender on its own was insuf-ficient to put respondents at ease. What is apparent is that shared statuses other than gender obviously influenced successful interviewing.

Power relations are intrinsic to understanding exclusivity and indeed some feminists claim that power relations are less of a problem in a woman-to-woman interview because women have the same structurally disadvantaged position in society. However, some feminists, whilst broadly supporting this position, have pointed to the drawbacks it might have for interviewing. Finch (1984) argues that shared sisterhood may give a false sense of security to women respondents, and may lead to them being 'too open' in the interview situation. Finch's case here rests on the assumption that the interview is inherently unequal and that control always rests with the interviewer. Respondent power is generally either underplayed or absent from accounts of research. Power and status that come 'with the job' are occasionally acknowledged, thus accounts of interviewing management of any kind and accounts of interviewing one's peers or 'seniors' are commonplace (cf. Platt 1981; Scott 1984, 1985). Often this is linked to the gender-related imbalance of power which is argued to exist when women are interviewing men in 'male-dominated settings' (Gurney 1985, 1991). However, only occasionally are deviations from the active/passive, dominant/subordinate model acknowledged (McKee and O'Brien 1983. 149) and 'ordinary' respondents are generally portrayed as powerless beings at the mercy of researchers.

However, in most research situations it would be more accurate to see the opposite as being the case, with the researcher very much dependent on the goodwill and co-operation of her/his respondent. My own experience sheds a different light on the power issue, for there are unique factors in the research situation which contradict the commonly held conception of researcher-respondent power. In fact, I can identify ways in which my respondents had the upper hand. The women respondents were in a different position to women in society at large. The unique setting in which these interviews were conducted allowed the women an element of control. The physical location of the study (in prison) meant that the women were on territory familiar to them. For example, they were able to engage in sexual banter from the relatively safe environment of the prison. In effect the more usual situation, where women are exposed to sexual harassment from men, was reversed so that I as a man became the object of sexual catcalls and innuendoes.

That the women co-operated willingly in the research leads me to my final point in this section, which is the importance of the personality and demeanour of the researcher. The willingness to co-operate is dependent to a large extent on *genuine empathy*. Indeed it seems curious that this aspect of the research process is continually overlooked or played down. On the one hand, as we have argued, the direct effects of essentialism limit access to different groups of participants, yet at the same time there is the tacit assumption that once 'in' as it were (and attention has been paid to details of sameness such as gender) a researcher will be able to draw information from any respondent. Yet we all know, that in everyday life, some people are easier to talk to and have a way of putting others at ease, whilst others seem to create barriers and irritate people without trying. Why should it be assumed that those wishing to do research are different? In a similar vein, I would challenge the view that women are better talkers and listeners than men in all cases.

Some authors have rightly pointed to the importance of having an interest not only in the topic which is being researched but also in the people who form the researched group. Buchanan, Boddy and McCalman (1988) speak of *genuine interest*. Shaffir (1991) states more clearly and honestly that initial and continued access often rests on the relationship between the interviewer and her/his respondents. He contends that

> '. . . successful entry to the research setting, and securing the requisite co-operation to proceed with the study, depend less on the execution of any scientific canons of research than upon the researcher's ability to engage in sociable behaviour that respects the cultural world of his or her hosts'. (p.73).

The researcher's personality has never been consistently recognised as a distinct aspect of the research process. Personality and demeanour are elusive qualities, and the assertion that they might be central to the whole process of research poses problems which most writers would appear reluctant to engage with. All interviews are performed within gendered contexts and it may be that some men who study women using in-depth interviews may confront formidable obstacles to rapport. However, in certain circumstances the gender difference may have little bearing or indeed might actually be of benefit. My contention here is not that we should therefore 'forget' gender issues within research or deny their influence upon the research process, but that the personality and demeanour of researchers may have far more bearing upon success or failure within interviewing than is usually acknowledged.[3]

Conclusion

In this chapter we have sought to describe the ways in which we have encountered essentialism within research. Our fields of research are very different and it is therefore interesting to see the similarities between our experiences in this respect. In this conclusion we summarise these common themes.

We have been concerned about the extent to which certain disciplines (Deafness research, disability studies, feminist research) emphasise the importance of epistemological privilege and how some authors appear keen to claim the 'right to know' based upon certain shared statuses. However, our own experiences of undertaking research stand in direct contrast to these edicts. Whilst it is distinctly 'unfashionable' to flaunt one's difference in public, there are underlying issues of academic freedom at stake if the problems raised in this chapter remain undisclosed and undiscussed.

We do not deny or refute the historical oppression of Deaf people by Hearing people or of women by men. We acknowledge the full weight of these oppressions and appreciate fully the bearing that these must have upon the research process. Our argument is with those people, (both researchers and respondents) who seek to emphasise 'ingroup' and 'outgroup' and by so doing place limits on what is and is not 'legitimate' to research. We offer our experiences therefore not as evidence of what is possible within hostile research climates but as texts for debate within the academic and practitioner communities.

Bibliography

Baker-Shenk, C. and Kyle, J. G. (1990) 'Research with deaf people; issues and conflicts', *Disability Handicap & Society*, Vol. 5 No. 1 pp.65-75.

Barnes C. (1996) Disability and the myth of the independent researcher, *Disability & Society*, Vol. 11. No. 1. pp 107-110.

Buchanan, D., Boddy, D. and McCalman (1988) 'Getting in, getting on, and getting out', in Bryman [ed.] (1988) *Doing Research in Organisations* Routledge pp.53-67.

Collins, P. H. (1990) *Black Feminist Thought Boston*: Unwin Hyman.

DeVault, M. (1990) 'Talking and listening from women's standpoint: Feminist strategies for interviewing and analysis' *Social Problems* Vol. 37 pp.96-117.

Finch, J (1984) ' "It's great to have someone to talk to": the ethics and politics of interviewing women', in Bell and Roberts (1984) *Social Researching: Politics, Problems, Practice*, Routledge and Kegan Paul pp.23-31.

Fishman, P. (1990) 'Interaction: The Work Women Do' in McCarl Nielsen, J. [ed.] *Feminist Research Methods: Exemplary Readings in the Social Sciences* London: Westview Press.

Fuller, R. and Petch, A. (1995) *Practitioner Research* Open University Press, Buckingham.

Gurney, J. N. (1985) 'Not one of the guys: the female researcher in a male-dominated setting', *Qualitative Sociology*, 8 pp.42-62.

Gurney, J. N. (1991) 'Female researchers in male-dominated settings: implications for short-term versus long-term research', in Shaffir, W. B. and Stebbins, R. A. [eds.] (1991) *Experiencing Fieldwork: An Inside View of Qualitative Research*, pp.53-61. Sage Publications Ltd

Hall, S., Held, D. and McGrew, T. (1992) (Eds.) *Modernity and its futures* Open University Press, Cambridge, UK.

Harris, J. (1995) *The Cultural Meaning of Deafness; Language, Identity & Power Relations*, Aldershot: Avebury.

Lee, R. M. (1993) *Doing Research on Sensitive Topics* London: Sage.

McKee, L. and O'Brien, M. (1983) 'Interviewing men: Taking gender seriously', in Gamarnikow, E. *et al.* (1983) [eds.] Heinemann Educational Books Ltd. pp.36-45.

Oakley, A. (1981) 'Interviewing Women: a contradiction in terms', in Roberts, H. [ed.] (1981) *Doing Feminist Research*, Routledge and Kegan Paul pp 30-61.

Oakley, A. (1987) 'Comment on Malseed' *Sociology* Vol. 21 No. 4 p.632

Padfield, M. and Proctor, I. (1996) 'The effect of interviewer's gender on the interviewing process: A comparative study' *Sociology* Vol. 30 No. 2 pp.355-66.

Paylor, I. (1995) *Housing Needs of Ex-Offenders* Aldershot. Avebury.

Platt, J. (1981) 'Interviewing one's peers', *Sociology* 15 pp.75-91.

Reinharz, S. (1992) *Feminist Methods of Social Research* New York: Sage.

Renzetti, C. M. and Lee, R. M. (1993) [eds.] *Researching Sensitive Topics* Newbury Park, Sage.

Ryan, T. (1993) 'Insider Ethnographies' *Senior Nurse* Vol. 13 No. 6 pp.36-9.

Scott, S. (1984) 'The personable and the powerful: gender and status in sociological research', in Bell and Roberts [eds.] (1984) *Social Researching: Politics, Problems, Practice*, Routledge and Kegan Paul pp.47-55.

Scott, S. (1985) 'Working through the contradictions in researching postgraduate education', in Burgess, R. G. [ed.] (1985) *Field Methods in the Study of Education*, Falmer Press pp.33-41.

Shaffir, W. B. (1991) Managing a convincing self-presentation: some personal reflections on entering the field, in Shaffir and Stebbins [eds.] (1991) *Experiencing Fieldwork: An Inside View of Qualitative Research*, Sage Publications Ltd. pp.72-82.

Smith, D. E. (1987) *The Everyday World as Problematic: A Feminist Sociology* Boston: Northeastern University Press.

Song, M. and Parker, D. (1995) 'Cultural Identity: Disclosing Commonality and Difference in in-depth interviewing' *Sociology* Vol. 29 No. 2 pp.241-56.

Warren, B. C. (1988) *Gender Issues in Field Research*, Qualitative Research Methods Series 9 Sage.

Wibberley, C. and Kenny, C. (1994) 'The case for interactive interviewing' *Nurse Researcher* Vol. 3 March pp.57-64

Williams, C. L. and Heikes, E. J. (1993)' The importance of researcher's gender in the in-depth interview: Evidence from two case studies of male nurses' *Gender and Society* Vol. 7 No. 2 pp.280-91.

Woodward, K. (Ed.) (1997) *Identity & Difference* Open University / Sage publications.

End Notes:

1. Essentialism is the insistence upon core characteristics as central in importance. Several authors discuss how essentialism has permeated the post-modern social experience. For example, essentialism in relation to identity is discussed by Woodward (1997 p.11) but there are many manifestations, particularly in relation to new social movements (ibid. p.24)

2. Throughout the chapter the term 'Deaf' refers to those people who use the British Sign language (BSL) and who have a positive (political) sense of Deaf identity. This term 'Deaf' was chosen by Deaf people as a means of demonstrating political allegiance and is distinct from the term used for the audiological condition 'deaf'.

3. Whilst not directly addressing the issue of personality Padfield and Proctor (1996) do explore other aspects of this question. Song and Parker (1995), on the other hand, expand the debate with a discussion about cultural identity encompassing multiple positioning of identity, closed identitites, and disidentitifications.

Chapter 4
Researchers and gatekeepers: no common ground?

Caroline McGee

The process of negotiating with gatekeepers to gain access to research subjects or agency files is probably the most overlooked but problematic of all stages in successfully completing a research project. If access to participants is denied, the research cannot survive without a complete change in direction such as examining publicly available, secondary source material. Gaining access to research participants when the research is of a sensitive nature needs careful planning and foresight particularly in order to include those from minority ethnic communities and disabled people who may be wary of research as another means of exploitation.

This chapter will draw on the techniques used by the author to negotiate access to research participants in three sensitive qualitative studies. The first was an attempt to hear directly from parents and particularly children about their experiences of being involved with the child protection system. This will be referred to as the child protection study. The second project examines the protection of children who have experienced domestic violence: the domestic violence study. The final study was designed to explore the physical and psychological strategies employed by women in order to survive sexual assaults: the rape study.

The role of the gatekeeper:
Taylor and Bodgan (1984) coined the term 'gatekeepers' to refer to those individuals within an organisation who control access to the setting or to people for the purposes of research. Gatekeepers are not always those who may be perceived as having power within an organisation as they vary in their apparent social and political power, from the receptionist or secretary screening out enquiries to managers or doctors, to the chief executive of an organisation (Barker *et al*. 1994).

Westcott (1996) suggests that the term 'protectors' might be more appropriate 'since although agencies and individuals do fulfil a "gatekeeping" role, most are motivated by concerns to protect the welfare of those for whom they are responsible' (p.27). While this particular protective function is certainly one of the roles of the gatekeeper, it is not the only one. Gatekeepers may also seek to protect workers from an examination of their competence, or they may fulfil this role individually for themselves. This does not imply that gatekeepers who act in this way are concealing incompetence, merely that the prospect of a researcher closely examining their work may make staff anxious, especially if they are unclear about the independent status of the researcher. Workers may wonder what the true purpose of this research is, is there a 'hidden agenda'? Will the outcome affect their job or promotion? Is this a preliminary activity to a cut-back exercise? Will it mean organisational changes? The researcher may empathetically understand these anxieties and seek to reassure gatekeepers on the aims of the research. It is also true that the researcher is unable to control how any agency may interpret the results of the research and choose to apply them.

In this situation, it is obvious that, rightly or wrongly, the researcher is perceived as having considerable power, in relation to the individual workers. The researcher may in fact be feeling powerless in the face of gatekeepers who are blocking access. An impasse will be reached if the researcher does not recognise the threat of this perceived power and address the issues of how the research could be used to harm individuals or the agency.

A further protective function of the gatekeeper is to protect the time or effort of oneself or another. It is understandable that in terms of time commitment research could be quite low down on staffs' priorities. This is one instance where it is important to be prepared to offer something back to the agency in return for participation, at the very least a copy of the findings and offering to run a workshop in the agency to feed back the results of the project. Meaningful incentives will help to counteract the investment of time or effort demanded by the researcher. For those wishing to involve social services departments in the research it is necessary to submit an application to the Research Group of the Association of Directors of Social Services (ADSS). This is a gatekeeping committee which critically evaluates the quality and relevance of proposed research and then makes recommendations to social services departments as to whether they should co-operate with the research. By assessing research proposals centrally, much time is saved by individual social services departments who have numerous requests to participate in research.

In summary, then, the gatekeeper may be fulfilling one or more protective functions:

- Shielding a vulnerable client group
- Ensuring negative issues do not arise regarding worker or agency competence
- Deflecting demands for time or effort from already pressured individuals.

In the domestic violence research, it was not unusual for all of these three elements to figure prominently in access negotiations. For example, a number of social services departments throughout the country were very keen to partic-ipate in the project. However, after careful consideration they felt that due to organisational restructuring they would be unable to participate, for the following reasons:

- Due to the pressures of reorganisation, workers might not be as readily available to support clients should issues arise directly from participating in the research (protecting vulnerable clients)

- Workers ' anxieties regarding the restructuring could be exacerbated by requests to have their professional practice scrutinised by the researcher (protecting individuals and the agency)

- During the restructuring, the agency would be concentrating on ensuring the smooth and effective running of the child protection service. (Protecting the time and effort of individuals.)

Histories and tensions

Just as it is now widely recognised that no researcher comes to a project in a completely objective manner so too is the dynamic between researcher and gatekeeper influenced by subjective motivations and history. It is important to know if there is a history of contact between the research organisation and the gatekeeping agency and to be aware of the nature of the relationship between the two agencies. A previous bad relationship does not necessarily mean that it will not be possible to proceed, merely that greater sensitivity will be needed in approaching that organisation. Similarly, a good working relationship between the two agencies does not necessarily mean that they will be willing to participate.

It is also important not to take the easy option of repeatedly approaching 'friendly' agencies to participate in research to the exclusion of other agencies. In addition to introducing possible bias into the research, it is unlikely that any organisation will be happy to be repeatedly asked to take part. In the child protection study, a number of agencies felt that they could not participate because their clients were in danger of becoming over researched. The agencies felt that this situation would not be beneficial for either the individual clients or the agency.

In all cases it is vitally important to agree, from the beginning, common aims and objectives of the research. It is not unusual for agencies, research participants, and the researcher to all have different expectations regarding the purpose and application of the research.

Hierarchies and hurdles

Negotiating access is not a one-off stage, it is an ongoing process which must be managed throughout the life of the research. In addition, there are many levels of access negotiations within each agency and each one of these levels is equally important. In order to gain access to participants through an agency, it is usually advised to start from the top and work your way down (Cowen and Gesten 1980), approaching senior managers first and, on their approval, beginning negotiations with workers. Burgess (1991) believes that such 'top down' advice makes several assumptions about gaining access: 'First, it suggests that access involves little more than strategy and tactics for getting into a research location. Second, it presents access as a one-off activity that prefaces the real work. Third, it suggests that gaining access is isolated from the researcher 's relationships and from the politics of social investigation' (p.43).

I would also recommend a less linear approach in that the first contact point should be an informal discussion of the research at the proposal stage with staff in order to incorporate their ideas into the project. This also enables the researcher to ascertain the structure of the particular agency hierarchy and how access can most effectively be negotiated. The researcher is then equipped with the names and roles of key individuals whom they should approach. This initial contact will, hopefully, give the researcher some idea of the politics at work within that organisation as well as more general background as to its function and aims which may indicate that it is not appropriate to include this agency.

Dingwall (1980) has referred to a hierarchy of consent which assumes that senior personnel have the right to give permission for more-junior staff to be studied. Gaining permission from any level to contact research participants does not by any measure guarantee actual access. Senior management may wish the agency to co--operate with the research but front-line workers may feel differently and can easily block access. Alternatively, workers may be enthusiastic about the project but management may not deem it appropriate and decide that the agency is not to take part.

In non-hierarchical organisations such as collectives, all members of the collective may act as gatekeepers and the researcher must be prepared for possible time delays until all the collective can meet to discuss the proposed research. In the case of collectives, they will often decide about research participation without referring the researcher to their management committee.

Similarly, when using the media or direct access to participants the idea of a professional hierarchical gatekeeping structure does not generally apply. Here the focus is very much on finding a named liaison person or persons and moving quickly to contact participants, otherwise the opportunity may be lost due to a changing media focus or staff changes. Another form of direct access to participants is the Internet and no doubt this media will be fully exploited by researchers by, for example, contacting people through user groups. At the present time this form of access is something of an unknown entity for social researchers but in time, no doubt, the benefits and pitfalls of this media will become more evident.

Ethics and consent

Gatekeeping is often viewed as an activity of professionals who give or withhold permission for their clients or clients' files to be researched. In reality, the professional gatekeepers merely allow the gates to be opened to the real gatekeepers, the research participants themselves or another person close to the participant. This level may involve different dynamics but is as crucial as any other aspect of gatekeeping. However, discussions around gaining access often end at the point where agencies become involved with the research and do not address how participants may operate as gatekeepers. Participants may fulfil this role in relation to their own involvement in the project, or they may control access to other possible participants as in the case of snowball sampling, where the researcher relies on those who are already involved to introduce her or him to others in the participant's network.

People who need a service from an agency may feel pressurised to participate because the agency is involved. People may believe that declining to take part in the research may mean that they are refused services by the agency. There may also be confusion as to the independent status of the researcher with regard to the agency. At this level, participants may not feel that they can refuse outright to take part but will avoid participation in other ways, such as not turning up for appointments, forgetting the answers to questions, or claiming not to know or to have any opinion. It is essential that the researcher is vigilant around the issues of *informed consent, assent, and dissent.* By *informed consent* is meant the agreement to participate in research, based on a true and full understanding of the proposed research activity. Consent must be freely given. By *assent*, in this chapter's context, is meant a child's indicated, verbal or non-verbal, willingness to participate based on a limited understanding of the proposed research activity. To obtain assent researchers must be satisfied that to the best of their ability that they have attempted to explain the purpose and process of the research in language suitable to the child's level of understanding. By the term *dissent* is meant an expressed wish not to participate in the proposed study. For younger children particularly, attention must be paid to non-verbal means of expression, especially discomfort or distress.

When the research participants are children another level of gatekeeping is introduced as the carers must usually give their consent in addition to the child. In the domestic violence study, it was clear that children were much more willing to participate than agencies expected they would be. Involving children in research, quite rightly, means that the levels of gatekeeping are raised.

Table 4.1 Types of access negotiation

METHOD	PROS	CONS
Top Down		
Obtain consent from management before discussing research with front-line staff	1. Some agencies may react better to this approach as staff will respond to a senior management dictate that the agency will facilitate the research 2. By first approaching senior managers, the researcher avoids slighting those with the most obvious power in the agency	1. Senior management may agree to participate in research, however staff may block access 2. A direct approach to the most senior person in the organisation may mean the researcher does not become aware of the politics of the particular agency and how that may affect access negotiations 3. The independent status of the researcher may be queried
Bottom up		
Approach workers for consent then seek permission from management	1. The researcher has early direct contact with those who are usually in a position to provide access to the prospective participants 2. The researcher is able to informally learn more about the role and politics of the organisation 3. The most senior person in the agency may not be the most appropriate to contact. The researcher will save time by being directed to the correct gatekeeper	1. Senior management may feel that the researcher has committed a breach of organisational etiquette by first approaching less senior staff. 2. Those in senior positions have the power to overrule decisions made by front-line workers *re* participating in the research 3. Staff may be unwilling to discuss the research until management has agreed to participate
Staggered		
Approach workers, then management, then workers again	1. Researcher has an opportunity to learn more about the organisation before approaching management 2. There may be a better chance of getting both front-line staff and management consent and interest in the project	1. Senior managers may feel initial discussions with workers should not have occurred until they had an opportunity to consider the research proposal 2. It is time consuming
Flooding		
Simultaneously using a wide variety of recruitment methods	1. Publicity about the research reaches a wider variety of prospective participants and thus helps to minimise bias 2. It enables a project to survive when key agencies are unable to become involved or sustain involvement in the research by reducing the dependency on a limited number of gatekeepers 3. Direct access methods (e.g displaying posters) reduce the number of gatekeepers 4. Can be used to boost the number of participants 5. Useful for reaching 'hidden' populations	1. Very labour and time intensive 2. Researcher has very little control over participant recruitment (e.g. timing of media ads) 3. May raise safety concerns for the researcher, particularly when investigating sensitive or taboo topics or when doing home interviews with participants recruited through public advertising 4. May attract vulnerable people who need support, and time must be spent identifying appropriate resources for them. This can also be emotionally draining on the researcher

However, it is important to be clear about who is being protected. For example, in the domestic violence study, mothers and children were contacted through a voluntary group and were enthusiastic about participating. On the day of the first interview the agency decided they could not facilitate access as they were unaware that the researcher wanted access to children and they could not give permission for that access. (This is despite having verbal and written material from the first contact clearly stating that the primary focus of the research was to interview children and young people.) Preliminary discussions with mothers at this agency highlighted one particular area of the agency's practice which gave cause for concern. It is possible that the managers wished to avoid further scrutiny. As the agency controlled physical access to this group of women and children it was not possible to involve them in the research despite the fact that they wanted to participate.

Contacts and changes

Particularly in research on sensitive topics it is common for the researcher to be introduced to the agency or prospective participant (or both) by a sponsor. Lee (1993) defines the three main roles of the sponsor as:

- a bridge – that is, providing the research with a link into a new social world. Lee (1993) points out that for research on sensitive topics, bridges may be necessary for the researcher to even make contact with 'deviant worlds' (p.131)

- a guide – that is a person who provides a map for the researcher through unfamiliar territory by, for example, explaining features of the setting which are confusing and helping the researcher avoid *faux pas*

- a patron – facilitates access simply by his or her association with the researcher, as this association helps to secure trust.

As access negotiations are an ongoing process, to ensure their success it is important that the researcher maintains links with more than one liaison person in the agency. It is simpler (and from the agency's viewpoint easier to accommodate) to have one key individual in each agency who is the liaison person. This is a precarious situation because if that person leaves the agency, or is off for some time, the researcher is left without any contact within the agency and may have to start the process of access negotiations all over again. Agencies generally have numerous requests to take part in research and there is no guarantee that anybody other than the link person will remember agreement being reached regarding the project.

The researcher should aim to get decisions in writing. It may be difficult to persuade overworked staff to take time to put things in writing, but the researcher can facilitate this process by typing up an agreement and sending it to the workers or managers for their signature with a stamped addressed envelope for its return. It is also advisable to make notes of telephone conversations with the gatekeeper and send a copy to them for information. These gestures are not hugely time consuming but can make an important difference where agency participation may be jeopardised.

Researcher characteristics

Shaffir (1991) states that despite his anxieties about gaining access he has generally found that (a) people are more co-operative about participating in the research than he anticipates, (b) this co-operation is less a reflection of the scientific merits of the research than a response to the researcher's personal attributes and (c) research always involves varying degrees of pretence and dissimulation.

Personal attributes are very important and as Burgess (1991) points out, researchers' ascribed characteristics such as age, sex, social class, social status, and ethnicity influence the extent to which access is granted or withheld. However, no matter how much individuals respond to the personal attributes of a researcher, if they do not feel the research is relevant or designed to empower rather than exploit individuals, then they will not participate. Additionally, I would question the belief that research always involves some amount of pretence and dissimulation. This is an area which has been addressed by many researchers, and honesty regarding the aims, methods, and outcomes of the research is crucial in conducting ethical research.

A number of studies have examined the influence of gender on gaining access to research settings. Gurney (1991) found that, as a female, conducting long-term research in a male-dominated setting did arouse some tensions. She also reports, however, that in short-term research being female may facilitate access as women are viewed as non-threatening. Parsons *et al.* (1993) found that interviewer experience is more important than gender when dealing with gatekeepers.

Stages involved in negotiating access
Stage one: formulating the research proposal
The process of gaining access to research participants is one which needs to be initiated during the formulation of the research proposal, not when the proposal has been agreed and funds are released. This step has a number of advantages:

- Those working in the field will often know if similar research is already under way which may indicate that a change of focus is needed

- If there is no interest from a number of agencies, then gatekeeping is going to be a problem and the viability of the research is questionable

- By contacting gatekeepers at this point, it enables the researcher to utilise his or her expertise at the design stage

- If agencies have an opportunity to input at the proposal stage it generates greater interest in the research and increases the likelihood of their participating fully later on

- Stating in the proposal that the research has the support of a number of relevant agencies may mean that approval is more readily given as it appears to be a well-designed proposal with practical relevance.

In the domestic violence study I contacted both academics and relevant agencies before finalising the research proposal. In this instance it seemed initially that the major voluntary organisation working in this area was considering carrying out similar research. By meeting and discussing it at the design stage repetition was avoided.

By contacting the relevant agencies, they were able to have some input into the research design, which meant that they had a vested interest in the success of the project, thus enabling access to it later on.

In the rape study, early contact with crisis counselling groups indicated that recruiting participants through such centres would be difficult due to the levels of crisis women were in at the point they made contact with these centres. Thus it was clear that a more creative approach to contacting participants would have to be undertaken and more time allocated to the process of negotiating gatekeepers.

Even where key agencies are clearly willing and able to participate in the research, access negotiations will inevitably take much longer than anticipated. The unexpected will happen and, while the researcher cannot anticipate entirely where stumbling blocks may arise, allotting a generous timescale to access negotiations at each stage of the project will provide some form of a research safety net.

Stage two: formulation of the research tools
While formulating the research tools, it is time to approach the gatekeepers again. When using in-depth interviewing or questionnaires, it is important to have the interview schedules checked by practitioners, particularly if the researcher is going to be asking sensitive questions. Workers will be able to comment not just on the suitability of the questions but also on the sensitivity or appropriateness of the wording. By using this approach it means that there are more 'safety checks' built into the study. It is essential that some time be taken to do this than cause distress to participants later.

Similarly, when requesting access to case-files or other records, discussions with gatekeepers will indicate whether or not the researcher is likely to glean the desired information from the records using these tools and whether agencies would be happy for their files to be scrutinised in this way. When researchers do not have practical experience in the area they are researching it is all the more important that gatekeepers be used in this manner. Having people from the relevant agencies on an advisory or steering committee will not fulfil the same function, as they will have a vested interest in seeing the research succeed. Gatekeepers will usually demand a higher threshold before accepting the research.

Most agencies, in line with their protective functions, will want to see the research tools and statements of ethics and confidentiality before facilitating access to their client group. Having practical input in the design of the tools means that there are less likely to be problems raised by gatekeepers later on. In addition, in later negotiations, it may lend credibility to the study to be able to say that particular agencies helped with designing the research tools.

In the child protection study a number of agencies were involved in the development of the research, for example, several NSPCC child protection teams helped with designing the interview schedules by providing practical social work input on the process of alleged child abuse investigations. In addition a major voluntary group commented on the design and wording of publicity materials and the research instruments. This group was then happy to encourage service users to participate.

Stage three: the pilot study
At this point a number of agencies should be involved with the research and to cut down on time these should be included in the pilot study. Agencies used in the pilot should be included in the main study as gatekeepers may feel that they have put a lot of work into the project only to be sidelined by being relegated to the pilot. The researcher must be clear with the gatekeepers about the role of the pilot, how many participants will be involved and within what time-scale it will be completed. Once the pilot study is under way it is time to begin negotiating access with other agencies so that there are no gaps between pilot and main stages. As indicated earlier, being able to say that a number of agencies are involved at this stage will facilitate further access. When revisions have been made to the research design following the pilot study, it is good practice to go back to the gatekeepers who contributed to the design of the tools and describe the changes that have been made and the reasons for these.

Stage Four: the main study
At the main study stage, the researcher must maintain a careful balance between fieldwork and fostering relationships with gatekeepers. When access is proceeding smoothly, it is easy to forget that unless time is spent talking with gatekeepers, there will be gaps in the access to different sites or people. When the research involves face-to-face interviews, at the point where an individual

participant indicates willingness to become involved in the research, it can often take two to three weeks to arrange a time suitable to both researcher and interviewee for the interview.

Stage Five: analysis and write up
Involving gatekeepers at this level can add to the theoretical richness of the project by providing ongoing feedback on the results of the study. Gatekeepers can contribute their experience to the analysis and ensure that the research has a practical application. In the context of 'grounded theory' (Strauss and Corbin 1990) involving gatekeepers at this stage can mean that any theory emerging from the analysis is kept firmly grounded in real-life experiences, particularly if participants themselves give feedback on the results. 'Because it [theory] represents that reality, it should also be comprehensible and make sense both to the persons who were studied and to those practising in that area' (Strauss and Corbin 1990, p.23).

Power in access negotiations

Just as the process of gaining access to research participants is a fluid and ongoing procedure, so too is the issue of power dynamics in access negotiations. Conceptualisations of the power dynamic in research typically focus on the power of the gatekeeper over the researcher and ultimately the outcome of the research project. However, the power dynamic is more complex than this. The notion of the hierarchy of consent mentioned earlier is just one example of how the issue of power in access negotiations is multifaceted. The gatekeeping agency as a whole has considerable power over the researcher in terms of facilitating access to clients or records and thereby may ultimately influence whether the project succeeds or fails. Individuals in that agency will have power to a greater or lesser degree; for example, senior personnel may obviously have power in terms of flatly refusing or immediately agreeing to be involved in the research, but they are not usually the people who will control day-to-day access to the client group or records. Individuals may find ways to hinder or facilitate that access without directly opposing the decisions of senior management. For example, in the domestic violence study, although senior management in one agency agreed to take part, there was obviously some reluctance from one middle manager. Rather than directly oppose the research (and the senior manager) he attempted to cancel a meeting with the researcher when she was five minutes late following a four hour drive to the meeting.

As raised earlier, individuals within the agency may perceive the researcher as being very powerful in that he or she may appraise their work negatively. There may be fears that the outcome of the research will be used to justify organisational changes which may cause anxiety on the part of the workers.

As the research progresses and access negotiations continue the power dynamics will change continually.

Using the media creatively to contact participants

Researchers' efforts regarding gatekeeping are usually concentrated on developing relationships with organisations who have most direct contact with the particular group the researcher is interested in. Generally this is the most appropriate method of contacting participants; however, at times a more diverse approach will be necessary, for example when researching 'deviant worlds' (Lee 1993) or when it is clear from early discussions with the agencies that they are unable to facilitate access. In the rape study I used a number of different means to contact prospective research participants for the following reasons:

- Early discussions with relevant agencies indicated that involving their service users in the research would be problematic

- Research has been criticised for relying too heavily on samples of rape survivors contacted through rape crisis centres as this group may differ significantly from those who do not contact such centres

- Survivors of rape can be particularly hard to involve in research therefore in order to achieve realistic numbers much effort needs to be invested in publicising the research.

Using the mass media to contact prospective research participants is often viewed as a last resort. However, this approach can be utilised very successfully by researchers as was the case with the rape study. Using the mass media in this study did prove fruitful but was time consuming and involved a lot of 'chasing'. When using the media to contact participants it is very important to have more than one liaison person in the agency as staff turnover may be quite high in the media business and the researcher may find that they have to negotiate and re-negotiate with different people who have no knowledge of agreements having been reached beforehand. There are ethical and pragmatic questions raised by contacting participants in this way also, for example, what does the gatekeeping agency want in return for facilitating access to participants? Will this affect the confidentiality and/or anonymity of those who took part? Will the researcher be able to cope if there are very large numbers of interested respondents? Do the media have any affiliations (especially political ones) or policies which could interfere with the research?

Maximising interest in the research

Sheffir and Stebbins (1991) found, unsurprisingly, that the chances of gaining access are increased when the researcher's interests appear to coincide with those of the research subjects, whereas rejection is more likely when gatekeepers do not understand what the researcher is doing and what he or she wishes to know.

In order to maximise interest in the research I have found the following methods work very well:

●   Involve gatekeepers and/or participants at the design stage

●   Consider how the process as well as the final outcome of the research may benefit those participating by

1. providing relevant information to participants. In the domestic violence study, this often meant answering queries about available research literature. While participants were clear that no emotional support could be offered by the researchers, they often phoned to request research information.

2. being willing to participate in training events or conferences without charge to those agencies participating in the study. Publicity about the research can then be circulated to others attending.

3. where appropriate, providing feedback to agencies participating. For example, in the domestic violence study, informal evaluations were offered to agencies who facilitated access to larger numbers of participants provided participant anonymity could be protected. Participants were aware from the beginning of the possibility of anonymous group feedback to the agency.

4. making a commitment to return to the agencies to run workshops to disseminate the findings. Although agencies may be provided with reports of the research, a more interactive environment to feedback to practitioners, policy makers, and managers is useful.

5. sending all individuals and participating agencies copies of the findings. Summary copies rather than full reports are easier to peruse and more accessible. This includes providing feedback to all ages and abilities of participants in a form suitable to the needs of the individuals.

Conclusion

Barker et al. (1994) point out that research can be viewed as "intrusive, critical and a challenge to the established way of doing things." (p 46). It can additionally be seen as a negative force which will disrupt the lives of vulnerable people by asking insensitive questions or crass interpretations of case material. No matter how sensitively and ethically a research project is designed there is always the possibility that it may cause distress. By including the expertise of gatekeepers from the design stage, there is less likelihood of this happening. Practitioners and researchers can work productively together to improve both academic knowledge and practice responses and workers are usually keen to see research being sensitively conducted which will aid their agency to improve their practice. By matching workers' enthusiasm for relevant research with realistic researcher demands of clients, individual workers, and the agency it is possible that substantial common ground can be reached between researchers and gatekeepers.

Bibliography

Barker, C., Pistrang, N. and Elliott, R. (1994) *Research Methods in Clinical and Counselling Psychology*. Chichester, Wiley.

Burgess, R. G. (1991) 'Sponsors, gatekeepers, members and friends' in Sheffir, W. B. and Stebbins, R. A. (eds.) *Experiencing Fieldwork: An Inside View of Qualitative Research*. Newbury Park, Sage.

Cowen, E. L. and Gesten, E. (1980) 'Evaluating community programs' in Gibbs, M. S., Lachennieyer J. R. and Sigal, J. (eds.) *Community Psychology*. New York, Gardner.

Gurney, J. N. (1991) 'Female researchers in male-dominated settings: Implications for short-term versus long-term research' in Shaffir, W. B. and Stebbins, R. A. (eds.) (1991) *Experiencing Fieldwork: An Inside View of Qualitative Research*. Newbury Park, Sage.

Lee, R. M. (1993) 'The Access Process in Research on Sensitive Topics' in Lee, R. M. (1993) *Doing Research on Sensitive Topics*. Newbury Park, Sage.

Parsons, J. A., Johnson, T. P., Warnecke, K. B. and Kaluzny, A. (1993) 'The effect of interviewer characteristics on gatekeeper resistance in surveys of élite populations' *Evaluation Review* 17(2), pp.131-43

Shaffir, W. B. (1991) 'Managing a convincing self-presentation: Some personal reflections on entering the field' in Shaffir, W. B. and Stebbins, R. A. (eds.) *Experiencing Fieldwork: An Inside View of Qualitative Research*. Newbury Park, Sage.

Sheffir, W. B. and Stebbins, R. A. (1991) 'Getting In' in Sheffir, W. B. and Stebbins, K. A. (eds.) *Experiencing Fieldwork: An Inside View of Qualitative Research*. Newbury Park, Sage.

Strauss, A. and Corbin, J. (1990) *Basics of Qualitative Research: Grounded Theory Procedures and Techniques*. Newbury Park, Sage.

Taylor, S. J. and Bodgan, K. (1984) I*ntroduction to qualitative research methods. The search for meanings*. 2nd Ed. New York, Wiley.

Westcott, H. L. (1996) 'Practising ethical and sensitive child protection research' *Practice* 8(4), pp.25-32.

Chapter 5
Researching ethnicity: experiences and concerns

Kusminder Chahal

The extensive academic literature available on all aspects of black and minority ethnic people's lives is a testament to the interest generated by a population group which is categorised as different. The debates on what label should be ascribed to classify these people have continued to flourish. However, what this research and 'identity' debates have achieved is highly questionable. Research of and for black and minority ethnic people continues to be dominated by white academics and researchers. With these points in mind, this chapter is, first, an attempt from a black researcher's point of view to explore the conceptual categories which punctuate research and language to describe or explain the black and minority ethnic population.

Second, it will explore how the debates on 'ethnicity' and 'culture' affect the research process and how research with communities who are seen as different is undertaken.

Categorisation of difference

How people are classified in any given society is a universal phenomenon and concern (Banton 1987a, D'Souza 1995). In contemporary Britain categorisation is part of an on going academic debate focusing on ethnicity, culture, and identity (see Modood, 1992). Academic debates about whether 'race' is relevant, how to define ethnicity, and what is the one term that will unite all oppressed people who are not white (Banton 1987b) tend to overshadow the possibility that people's lives are not necessarily fashioned by a political identity. The ascription of all-inclusive identities is increasingly becoming determined by professionals who continue to provide new names (and possibly meanings) to people who often find these of little use in their day-to-day lives (Modood 1992).

Banton (1987a) shows that the concept of 'race' has changed over time and that the analytical term 'race' is problematic. Yet, although 'race' as a category has been discredited it still continues to be used widely in academic circles, thus providing it with a spurious legitimacy. The extensive use of ethnicity since the 1980s can be said to have taken the place of 'race' as the concept which is used to think of a form of human difference (Smaje 1995). Thus 'race' has become equivalent to 'ethnicity' (Ballard and Kalra 1994, Banton 1988) and 'ethnic' in everyday language. However, the analytical terms 'ethnicity' and 'race' have very different meanings (Bradby 1995, Miles 1989).

The adjective 'ethnic' has become synonymous with 'minority ethnic people'. This reduces what ethnic or ethnicity means to a descriptive difference. Similarly, the often used term 'non-white' by white, black, and minority ethnic professionals is used to describe colour difference (for example in research documents and as a self-description). Yet these descriptive terms cover a degree of complexity. For example, a survey in Derbyshire (Ethnic Minorities Health Needs Group 1995) found that travellers felt that the main determinant for improving their health was less racial harassment. The experience of discrimination and oppression was not determined by the colour of skin but, more importantly, by being a minority within a majority culture. Bradby (1995) notes:

'Everybody has ethnicity, but those who are of the majority ethnicity are not usually forced to think about it.'

However, if ethnic boundaries are fluid and imprecise (Senior and Bhopal 1994) when and how does ethnicity become 'ethnicity'? In other words, the assertion 'everybody has ethnicity' is applying a label before it has been discovered. If the majority community in their daily lives 'are not usually forced to think about it' how then is their ethnicity important? Indeed, it needs to be asked that if those who represent the majority ethnicity in contemporary Britain are 'white', how does this explain what the majority ethnicity is?

Further, the issue of labelling (conveniently hidden behind the more academic 'identity') in research of black and minority ethnic people has been promoted by those in positions of influence and power. But the true experts of their identity construction in different social situations are the subjects of research – namely black and minority ethnic people. Rarely are these people asked how they describe themselves (apart from in a close manner best illustrated by the Census classifications and in job applications for a crude measure of equal opportunity). I certainly have no knowledge of being consulted on whether I was a coloured, ethnic minority, minority ethnic, visible minority, person of colour, and now just an ethnic or non-white. Indeed, the use of non-white in recent research and newspaper reporting is profoundly offensive but also insightful both as a research category and as an imposed classification of identity. It has been noted:

'The realities of people of colour are never considered as legitimate standards of generalisation to Eurocentric realities. Imagine having a social science with cultural standards of generalisation that encourage researchers to apply what they have found in the process of studying Afro-Americans to white populations' Stanfield (1993:28)

Thus in the British context, we could argue that the use of non-white as a classification of experience and as a subject for research highlight how Eurocentric the social sciences still are. Indeed, why are we unable to use the term 'non-black' in research documents? The term 'white' (couched behind majority ethnicity) still appears to be the standard bearer of all measures within the process of social science research.

Defining ethnicity, and particularly being able to incorporate self-defined ethnicity, for operational purposes, is very difficult. Ethnicity as an identity is fluid, the notion of an 'ethnic identity' will vary according to political, geographical, and social changes (Senior and Bhopal 1994). Thus the content of what constitutes ethnicity is likely to change according to external conditions and individual perceptions as well as the context within which the question of identity is asked. It is obvious that the use of the term 'ethnicity' is problematic in everyday language and in developing research protocols. However, it has been argued that the term 'ethnicity' has been associated with breakdown of 'black solidarity' by emphasising the divisions within the minority ethnic groups in Britain (Bradby 1995, Ahmad 1989).

The term 'black' can be regarded as a euphemism created by liberal egalitarians to create a positive identity amongst minority ethnic groups to oppose racism. In reality 'black' is not used consistently both as an analytical or descriptive concept:

> 'The inherent difficulties in the idea of 'black' are evidenced by the fact that few Asian, black nor white people use this term consistently. Black people, for example, when speaking of Asians refer to them as such; when speaking of themselves and Asian they use the term 'black'; and when speaking only of themselves do not see themselves as a sub-group of 'black' but as the black community' (Modood 1992: 20).

It is difficult to argue for a collective identity for all non-white people under the banner 'black'. Given ethnicity is a socially constructed phenomenon (Senior and Bhopal 1994) the logical conclusion would be that so are 'white' and 'black'. In fact can we talk of a 'white' collective identity. Irish and Jews have been oppressed, stigmatised, and racialised as much as the contemporary minority groups (Holmes 1991). There is evidence to suggest that the health status and utilisation of services of the Irish are not comparable with the whole population of England and Wales. For example, Smaje (1995) highlights that coronary heart disease mortality is raised for men and women born in Ireland as well as the Indian subcontinent in comparison with gender-specific rates for the whole population of England and Wales. Is it, therefore, possible to talk of the Irish joining the ranks of 'black' because black is:

'A declaration of struggle for equality and justice. It is an acknowledgement of similar experience of racism and racial discrimination. . . . Above all it is a positive statement' (Ahmad 1989).

Although the Irish and Jewish communities do experience racism they are able to take on being white in most situations. Thus being black is part of being visible in a racialised society. It has been claimed that 'a considerable part of sociology consists of cleaning up the language in which common people talk of social and moral problems' (Hughes 1952). Definitions of ethnicity (e.g., Cashmore 1988, Senior and Bhopal 1994, Bradby 1995) are used to define people and situations for research. How well this has helped to clean up the language regarding the classification of black and minority ethnic people and the (mis)use of the term ethnicity is questionable.

Researching ethnicity
It has been argued that ethnicity has been 'rediscovered' (Richardson and Lambert 1986) but there has been no question of when and how it was lost. Richardson and Lambert state (1986:55) that the reorientation in academic studies towards a greater emphasis on ethnicity has been a welcome addition to the race relations literature. They also observe that from the 1960s onwards there was a concerted effort to map out the field of 'ethnic studies', and that this resulted in 'extremely valuable' ethnographic studies of the 'communities concerned'.

The 'communities concerned' were 'new commonwealth migrants'. The two examples of ethnographic studies given by Richardson and Lambert were on the Pakistani and West Indian communities. They point to 'the dangers of assuming that the migrant culture is homogeneous' yet there is no mention that the West Indies are a collection of islands some at least 1,000 miles from each other, each with its own sense of culture and identity. In addition, it seems that some sociologists have used the concept of ethnicity to talk of culture and identity of different groups. It needs to be argued that if ethnicity can be reduced to culture and identity then why are these terms not used to replace the 'ethnicity' label?

Academic discourse has often been accused of being ethnocentric when writing about ethnicity (CCCS 1988). Part of this might be because ethnicity is a difficult term to define (Bradby 1995). However, another potential reason is that ethnic and even cultural studies tend to look at difference and in this way ethnicity begins to equal difference. This is obvious in two ethnographic studies undertaken in London.

Examples of classifying research

Two studies undertaken in London in the early 1980s on health and illness (Cornwell 1984 and Donovan 1986) exemplify the methodological, epistemological and political issues surrounding the study of 'ethnicity'. Donovan's thesis is concerned with the perceptions and experiences of health, illness, and healthcare of 30 people of Afro-Caribbean and Asian descent (1986:xi). Cornwell's enquiry is about 24 people who live in East London with the aim of understanding these people's ideas and theories about health, illness and, health services (1984:1).

Both the studies are of relevance to understanding how people make sense of (ill) health. They are located in the same geographical area (London) and are both based on research undertaken for a PhD. However, that is where the similarity ends. Donovan highlights in her abstract that the people she is studying have an ethnicity. Cornwell is merely enquiring into the lives of a given number of people and gives no indication that she is studying 'an ethnic group'. How can Cornwell study twenty four people (all white) who seem to have no ethnicity and belong to no ethnic group, without reference to their racialised status yet Donovan is compelled to state whom she is studying?

Cornwell's study could quite easily be a study of an ethnic group. For example, she refers to a strong sense of community in Bethnal Green, the area in which she undertook her research. She states that this sense of community is apparent in a dislike of what is different. This is a clear example of an ethnic group as defined by Schermerhorn (1970). But there is no trace of this study being about health and ethnicity. It is a mainstream thesis about people's lives.

The distinction between the two studies is completed by the varying cataloguing given by the British Library Cataloguing in Publication Data. Donovan's book is catalogued 'Minorities – Health and hygiene – England – London'. Whilst Cornwall's book is described as 'Medical care – Great Britain – Public Opinion – Case Studies'.

The difference in the classification could not be more diverse. It would seem that ethnicity and the study of it in the social sciences are used to refer to the ubiquitous 'other'. There is very little acknowledgement that localised studies about white people can also be described as studies of ethnicity. Yet there is a preoccupation with 'getting it right' in terms of categorisation of black and minority ethnic people. It is also acknowledged that this is less the case now than it was when Cornwell and Donovan undertook their respective studies.

The sociological issue that might need further investigation is not whether people have an ethnicity but how it is used and how it influences people's day-to-day lives, if at all. Or are there other social phenomena which might more accurately reflect people's actions and responses? Thus in Cornwell's thesis, unemployment and the changing economic base are one influence on people's lives. In Donovan's, however, the whole text reads 'ethnicity' and there is no real development on how people live their lives. Her assumption is that all people have an ethnicity and so this must be relevant to them.

Moerman (1974:62) argues that 'the preferring of any identification should be a problematic phenomenon, not a comforting answer'. His central thesis is that the research dilemma should not be 'who' are a given group, but when, how, and why the identification of that group is important. Thus ethnicity as an analytical and descriptive term should be questioned and not accepted as fact. In this sense social science, and particularly sociology, may get closer to the notion of 'similarities' rather than the over-studied 'difference'. The study of 'ethnicity' could be, as Moerman argues, about how social scientists describe and analyse the ways in which 'ethnic identification devices' are used and not to adopt them as explanations.

Experiences from and in the field
The above discussion on ethnicity has an immediate bearing and impact on the research process with minority ethnic communities. The legacy of a long and drawn-out debate about ethnicity means that minority ethnic people are seen as different with a dramatically different set of problems from wider society. In other words they are continually marginalised, set apart, seen as the 'other'. This is apparent in a number of ways which are discussed below.

The identity of the (black) researcher
I was recently asked by a colleague if I was a researcher or a black researcher. It was not as if I had never had to think about this before whilst undertaking research, particularly with black communities. However, rather than this question having a straightforward answer it is complicated by the fact that if a researcher has an identity then surely that identity changes according to the research process. Thus, am I a 'black researcher' when working on 'black' issues and a 'researcher' when undertaking other research which does not concern ethnicity or racism? By identifying myself as a 'black researcher' do I affect the way in which I approach the research subject and what I find?

In my career as a researcher I have not met any black researchers working on non-black issues yet I have met many white researchers/academics working on black issues. That is not to say that black researchers undertaking mainstream research do not exist but it does seem that they are more likely to be employed to undertake specialist research rather than be involved in mainstream research.

As a researcher, my career started in 1991 investigating the nature and extent of racial harassment (Chahal 1992). This was a one-year funded project and very quickly my naïvety was broken by the realisation that if I was to progress in my chosen profession I should be careful of not pigeon-holing myself in only 'black research'. The notion of pigeon-holing had been introduced to me by other black professionals, particularly in social services, who felt marginalised because they were not seen as 'mainstream' workers but occupying a specialism. I did not want a specialism imposed on me by others. Rather I wanted to develop a specialism from my own experiences which I could claim my own and not because of preconceived views of what I should do. With these early thoughts in my career I became conscious of what I was applying for.

However, now equipped with a range of experiences of research and social issues I still find that I am more likely to be short-listed for 'black' research projects than any other yet I have a diversity of experience. The consequence of this is that I am more likely to apply for 'black' projects than others because I feel I have an increased chance of being selected for interview. Ironically, therefore, I have become a specialist in black research without having chosen such a path.

The process of social research tends to politely ignore that the experiences of the researcher both in the field and of the field are crucial findings in themselves. Although there is an issue of disclosure relevant to this form of reflection, the experience of the researcher is fundamental in identifying the layers of power intrinsic in social research, between researcher-researched and researcher-funding agencies (or steering groups). Bhavnani (1988) notes that the analysis of power should be part of all research even when this is not the primary focus of it.

Social research among black and minority ethnic communities

It would not be difficult to argue that minority ethnic communities are an over-researched group and that the output from all this activity fuels a 'race' industry. More practically we could ask how useful all this activity has been in promoting change, developing services, or improving access to services:

'For some years I have felt that in Britain the voluminous research on the health of ethnic minorities has not paid the dividends in terms of better services . . . indeed I cannot recall a single solid advance in our understanding of the cause of disease which can be attributed to such research' (Bhopal 1992:51).

It has further been observed:

'Health research on black people is concentrated in a small number of areas, largely of clinical interest. Within this it has often concentrated on exotica. One can begin to make sense of this concentration by looking at the processes involved in the construction of this research. One reason may be the continued fear of and fascination with what in the West have been defined as exotic people, exotic customs and exotic diseases . . . cultural quirks or peculiar diseases are more often the subject of research than racism within medicine . . . ' (Ahmad 1993:23).

We could easily replace the references to health with any other social issue. Undertaking research with minority ethnic communities would clearly seem to be a viable activity. But why such interest and what has it achieved?

' . . . academic research which has amassed ample evidence of racial discrimination and disadvantage has produced no tangible results or committed and positive action to attack the fundamental roots of the situation – racism. This divorce of research from committed action is understandably viewed with increasing suspicion and hostility by black people who are the objects of more and more research' (Pearson 1986:100).

Research based on the variable ethnicity should be viewed with caution as expressing a particular need at the expense of a universal need across all communities. Although specific needs may be highlighted around language, religion, or even diet, the expression of need is usually not different from people of all backgrounds. For example, a study on housing needs of south Asian communities found that:

'The housing requirements of the Asian community in Rochdale are the same as those of the general population, that is, a decent roof over their heads, in an area of their choice, at a price they can afford' (Athar 1989:1).

Studies have also shown that comparisons across ethnic groups within south Asian communities may not be the most important variable to consider when analysing research data (Rai 1995). The issue of selecting appropriate variables for research within south Asian communities (for example, religion, country and region of origin, language) would appear to be an important factor for consideration in the design of some research studies but actually yields very little in terms of insight of the one under investigation. For example, a study conducted in Leicester to identify the economic and social constraints under which south Asian women (Gujarati- and Punjabi-speaking from Sikh, Hindu, and Muslim backgrounds) in hosiery, knitwear, and other clothing industries work reported that:

> 'there were no significant differences in the views of the four ethno-
> linguistic groups surveyed' (MORI, 1993:iii).

Similarly, a health needs assessment undertaken in Crawley (Chahal 1996) with south Asian communities found no difference across region or religion with regards to views on accessing services, perceptions of health, or satisfaction with services. However, the survey found massive differences across the gender divide within the communities under research on issues such as the comparable status of physical and mental health of men and women, suggesting that the most important research variable was gender and not ethnicity or religion. This difference, though, is rarely looked upon because it does not focus on ethnicity. The general problem seems to be that research commissioners and designers fall into the recurrent trap of pre-defining a group of people and then setting out to investigate that group of people, rather than recognising when and how ethnicity is relevant in relation to the subject under study.

Investigating differences across minority ethnic communities is largely a measure of which group is closely fitting or varying from the 'white standard'. Needs assessment with 'white' communities does not have to concern itself with variables such as religion or ethnicity because the focus of attention is not on highlighting differences between people but on their perception of need based on knowledge as local people.

This knowledge that minority ethnic people possess is forgotten and replaced by pre-defined characteristics of the research cohort. Certainly, there are differences across the range of ethnic groups but these could be explored and developed in conjunction with the population make-up of the local area. How useful ethnicity as a variable is in improving access to a service or as part of a research strategy is debatable. The reality is that research with minority ethnic communities is not a mainstream, incorporating phenomena; rather it is piecemeal, tailored to political agendas, and exclusive.

Developing a research agenda
Although minority ethnic communities have been the focus of much research, the location of this activity is in specific geographical areas. Where there is a sizeable and visible minority ethnic population, research and community based projects and courses proliferate. In areas where the presence of minority ethnic communities is small there is a noticeable absence of such activity. The standard response to this difference is that 'there is no problem here because it is a small community'. In this way minority ethnic communities become problematised and relevant research becomes problem led. In low-density areas of minority ethnic settlement black communities are more likely to be isolated (e.g., Mann-Kler 1997) and there are more likely to be acute issues of services access and development because these communities are largely neglected and ignored. If there is no research-led service development then minority ethnic communities will not only be ignored in the planning of local services but also in any research sampling arising from surveys or consultations.

The development of a research agenda *vis-à-vis* minority ethnic communities is based on inappropriate assumptions. First, similar to the immigration debate of the 1960s and 1970s, commissioning research is based on a crude 'numbers game'. The larger the numbers of minority ethnic settlement in specific areas the more political the will to undertake needs assessments. Thus, even the specific dynamic of developing a research agenda problematises minority ethnic communities and categorises them into research and non-research subjects. At the very local level, my general experience has been that local authority commissioned research is about containment rather than effecting change.

Second, the 'numbers game' adversely affects minority ethnic communities living in isolated areas because they are usually not considered for health and social service programmes, link workers, or the development of community based facilities. For example, I was asked recently to undertake a feasibility study for establishing an Asian women only health course. Suggesting that this should be done in an area of low ethnic minority population it was questioned whether recruitment would be possible. The feasibility study I undertook not only showed a group of women who wanted to attend any course but also the fact that they felt ignored in service development and had very little made available to them in terms of encouraging and providing information about service access. Third, they felt they were not represented or had a voice.

In the name of 'good race relations' research and community development in areas of 'high density minority ethnic settlement' is quite a pervasive activity. This is largely a political response to fill gaps in knowledge in a local area, but not necessarily one of taking action. However, in areas of low density minority ethnic settlement there is little research or community development reinforced by the official line 'we have good race relations' and 'there are no problems here'. Thus in the name of a *mythical* relationship very little is undertaken or achieved. Or what is undertaken is tokenist, short-term, reactive research or development work. Promoting or preserving good race relations is used as a pretext to both doing nothing or very little (in low density minority ethnic areas) or undertaking reactive research (in high density areas).

Research design
As discussed earlier in this chapter the social sciences have problematised 'ethnicity' rather than clarified its usage and meaning. This has direct consequences on the design and method adopted by social research in its over-pursuit of finding out about minority ethnic communities. The over-emphasis on 'ethnicity' has allowed minority ethnic individuals to be seen not as people but as a group which represents a way of life that is different within British society. The fact that these people are human, social, and moral beings is side-stepped to enhance academic careers based on Eurocentric social science measures (Stanfield 1993).

Social research generally views minority ethnic people as the 'other' to general society and, therefore, a legitimate target for marginalised research focusing on difference and 'exotica'. Where minority ethnic people are represented in national mainstream surveys, they are usually added on as a booster sample. However, in general, minority ethnic people are ignored in mainstream surveys both at the local and national levels. For example, a postal survey undertaken in West Sussex (Singleton and Turner 1994) with elderly people, made little attempt to incorporate the views of the Asian elderly and thus they were denied a say in the development of strategic service planning.

It is easier to ignore and exclude minority ethnic people in mainstream research than to attempt to incorporate them. The power of positivism effectively excludes the voice of the minority to the advantage of the standard bearer:

'Too many studies are published . . . that are rooted in white populations and samples, with, perhaps, short notes explaining the reasons for excluding people of colour, whose presence in the study would complicate the analysis' (Stanfield, 1993:27).

Rai (1995:45) discovered that, rather than attempt to develop innovative methodological approaches, research organisations excluded minority ethnic communities because of methodological problems and possible higher costs.

More importantly, Rai found that minority ethnic communities just did not feature in research designs. They do not feature because their views are less important than the 'white standard' when the research question or study is about general issues.

Where minority ethnic people can be seen as being different or problematic, research is undertaken exclusively about them. A clear example of this is the large number of localised research on the nature and extent of racist harassment (see for example Chahal 1992, Hesse 1992). Why is it important to undertake such a range of geographically based research on racist harassment. Why do minority ethnic people have to continue to substantiate that they are the victims of racism? Compare the research undertaken on racist harassment with other forms of violence, such as domestic violence or child abuse. There is no consideration in the child abuse literature, for example, that it occurs more in some geographical areas than others. Yet the experience of racism is continually questioned and localised and in this way becomes ignored or termed anecdotal.

The contradiction in the research process is that although minority ethnic people are ignored in general mainstream research, the reliability of a study is questioned when no comparative white samples or populations are used in research on black and minority ethnic communities. Certainly I have had experience of being criticised and had the utility of findings questioned because of not incorporating a non-black sample. The Home Office (1981), in recognising that black and minority ethnic people experience and suffer racist harassment measured the level of experience against a white comparative sample. This obvious contradiction within the social research process questions the validity of black and minority ethnic people's experiences:

> 'The subtle evolutionary presumptions underlying such criticism are more than apparent. People of colour in many social science circles are not relevant enough to stand on their own two feet in analysis; unless they are compared with whites, they have no value in important social science circles' (Stanfield 1993:27).

Rather than seeing black and minority ethnic people as full members of society, they are firmly fixed as marginal to the wider pursuit of social research. The consequence is that the focus on difference by cultural pluralists denies certain facts of black and minority ethnic people's experience – that ultimately difference is expressed in racism (Pearson 1986).

Conclusion
Researchers very rarely reflect on their experiences as part of the total output of a research document. Yet this could be actively promoted as a legitimate goal of social research. Stanfield (1993:26) observes that black academics

with 'liberating views on racism' are generally ignored by the academic communities. Only acceptance of the *status quo* and current trends allows incorporation into this professional community.

Quite simply, the social sciences and social research expect black researchers/academics to accept their standards rather than question the assumptions that white, European social sciences are built on. There are still too few black and minority ethnic academics/researchers leading debates and research in the so-called race relations industry and even fewer in mainstream social sciences.

Rather than continuing to hide behind drawn-out debates about culture and identity, the social sciences need to radically reassess the status of 'ethnic studies' as a separate area of study and within the broad field of human sciences. If ethnicity is to continue as a marginal subject then perhaps academic and service providers alike should admit a crucial research finding – that right on their doorstep they confirm and reproduce the position of black and minority ethnic people in contemporary Britain.

References

Ahmad, B. (1989) 'Self definition and black solidarity' in *Social Work Today*, 11 May 1989

Ahmad, W. I. U. (ed.) (1993) *'Race' and health in contemporary Britain* Buckingham, Open University Press

Athar, M. (1989) *Survey of the Asian Community's Housing Needs* Rochdale, Asian Special Housing Initiative Agency

Ballard, R. and Kalra, V. S. (1994) *The Ethnic Dimension of the 1991 Census: A Preliminary Report*. Manchester: Census micro data Unit, University of Manchester.

Banton, M. (1987a) *Racial Theories* Cambridge, CUP

Banton, M. (1987b) The battle of the name *New Community*, xiv (1/2), 170-5

Banton, M. (1988) *Racial Consciousness* London, Longman

Bhavnani, Kum-Kum (1988) Empowerment and social research: Some comments *Text*, 8 (1/2), 41-50

Bhopal, R. (1992) 'Future research on the health of ethnic minorities: back to basics: a personal view' in Ahmad, W. I. U. (ed.) *The Politics of 'Race' and Health* Bradford, Race Relations Research Unit, University of Bradford and Bradford and Ilkley Community College

Bradby, H. (1995) 'Ethnicity: Not a black and white issue. A research note' *Sociology of Health and Illness* 17(3), pp405-17

Cashmore, E. E. (1988) *Dictionary of Race and Ethnic Relations* London, Routledge

Centre for Contemporary Cultural Studies (CCCS) (1988) *The Empire Strikes Back: Race and Racism in 70s Britain* London, Hutchinson

Chahal, K. (1992) *Hidden from View: Racial Harassment in Preston* Preston, Preston Borough Council

Chahal, K. (1996) *Minority Ethnic Health in Crawley* West Sussex Health Authorities (Unpublished)

Cornwell, J. (1984) *Hard earned lives* London, Tavistock Publications

Donovan, J. (1986) *We don't buy sickness, it just comes* London, Gower

D'Souza, D. (1995) *The end of racism* New York, The Free Press

Ethnic Minorities Health Needs Group (1995) *Travellers in North Derbyshire; report of the Travellers Health Questionnaire*

Hesse, B., Rai, D. K., Bennett, C. and McGilchrist, P. (1992) *Beneath the surface: racial harassment* Aldershot, Gower

Holmes, C. (1991) *A tolerant country? Immigrants, refugees and minorities in Britain*. London, Faber and Faber

Home Office (1981) *Racial attacks* London, HMSO

Hughes, E. C. and Hughes, H. M. (1952) *Where peoples meet: racial and ethnic frontiers* Glencoe, Illinois, The Free Press

Mann-Kler, D. (1997) *Out of the shadows: An action research report into families, racism and exclusion in Northern Ireland* Belfast, Barnados

Miles, R. (1989) *Racism* London, Routledge

Modood, T. (1992) *Not easy being British: Colour, Culture and Citizenship* Stoke-on-Trent, Trentham Books

Moerman, M. (1974) 'Accomplishing Ethnicity' in Turner, R (ed.) *Ethnomethodology* Harmondsworth, Penguin, pp54-68

MORI (1993) *Asian women workers in the hosiery, knitwear and clothing industries* Leicester City Council

Pearson, M. (1986) 'The politics of ethnic minority health studies' in Rathwell, T. and Phillips, D. (eds.) *Health, 'race' and ethnicity* Kent, Croom Helm Ltd pp100-16

Rai, D. (1995) *In the margins: current practices in qualitative social research with Asian communities* Hull, Social Research Publications, School of Policy Studies, University of Humberside

Richardson, J. and Lambert J. (1986) *The Sociology of Race* Ormskirk, Causeway Books

Schermerhorn, R. (1970) *Comparative ethnic relations* New York, Random House

Senior, P. A. and Bhopal, R. (1994) 'Ethnicity as a variable in epidemiological research' *British Medical Journal*, Vol. 309, 1994: 327-30

Singleton, N. and Turner, A. (1994) *The health needs of elderly people in Crawley and Horsham: Results of the postal survey* Crawley, Crawley Horsham Trust

Smaje, C. (1995) *Health, 'race' and ethnicity: making sense of the evidence* London, King's Fund Institute

Stanfield II, J. H. (1993) 'Epistemological considerations' in Stanfield II, J. H. and Dennis, R. M. (eds.) *Race and Ethnicity in Research Methods* California, USA, Sage

Chapter 6
Protection or empowerment: an exploration of the dilemmas involved in research with children

Maria Ruegger

This chapter highlights recent shifts in policy and ideas concerning the status and rights of children to be consulted about matters that concern them, particularly in relation to their inclusion in research where the aim is to acquire knowledge about children. The author explores the reasons that might account for the barriers that are frequently erected to prevent access to this group through an examination of two underlying value positions that are often in conflict: the protectionist and the liberationist – themes which emerged from empirical work undertaken in relation to her research on Children's Perceptions of the Guardian ad Litem Service.

A major theme for social work generally, and child care in particular, during the eighties and nineties has been that of 'empowerment'. The practice of empowerment is concerned with altering the balance of power between groups or individuals in favour of those who are traditionally in the weaker position. Children as a group are often powerless by virtue of their dependence on adults and their lack of resources, with the result that traditionally they have not been consulted about their needs and experiences; adults have made decisions and choices on their behalf based on their own ideas about what children think, feel, and need. In professional social work practice there has been a recent move towards thinking about the involvement of children in decision making at some levels, for example attendance at case conferences and statutory reviews to eliciting children's views on individual arrangements that must be made for them and establishing accessible complaints procedures.

These developments in social work practice can, at the macro level, be understood in the context of the wider changes in law and social policy which reflect similar ideologies and shifts in emphasis in the way in which children are viewed as members of society. In 1989 Britain became a signatory to the United Nations Convention on the Rights of the Child. Article 12 states that

'States Parties shall assure to the child who is capable of forming his or her own views the right to express those views freely in all matters affecting the child, either directly or through a representative of an appropriate body, the views of the child being given due weight in accordance with the age and maturity of the child'.

All the other articles in the convention hinge on the recognition that children should be consulted in all important decisions that have to be taken in regard to them. The Children Act (1989) embodies this principle and requires courts to have regard to

> 'the ascertainable wishes and feelings of the child concerned (considered in the light of his age and understanding'. (Section 1(3)(a).)

In the principles and practice guide which accompanies the act, principle number 25 states:

> 'Young people's wishes must be elicited and taken seriously. Even quite young children should be enabled to contribute to decisions about their lives in an age appropriate way. . . . Young people in care should be given the chance to exercise choice and if they are unhappy about decisions or placements, they should have the opportunity to be heard and taken seriously'. (Department of Health, 1990 p12).

In the field of social research too there has been a growing recognition that children's views can be elicited directly on a whole range of issues that affect them. However, despite the many studies that have been conducted with a view to learning about children and their lives, it is still comparatively rare for researchers to collect data directly from this group. Traditionally, research concerning children collects data from adults, such as parents and teachers, rather that asking children directly about their experiences. Trends towards the direct involvement of children in research are only just beginning to be seen across a range of related disciplines in the field of social research (Alderson, 1993; Mayer, 1994). Sociologists Morrow and Richards (1996, p92) suggest that a 'small but significant amount of activity appears to be developing into a discrete discipline within sociology, a sociology of childhood'. In research with a specific social work perspective the trend towards consulting children also appears to be moving forward, albeit slowly, as suggested by the proportion of studies commissioned by the Department of Health programme of research in child protection, (Department of Health, 1995), where data was obtained directly from children.

Evidence from those studies in which children have been interviewed for the purposes of research (see for example Alderson (1993) and Sharland *et al.* (1995)), suggests that children have a valid contribution to make, and that they actively welcome the opportunities afforded by research to comment on legal and investigative processes in which they have been involved. Whilst these positive experiences are likely to mean that the direct involvement of children in research is set to become an ever more common feature, it is however a developing field and one which is still in its infancy. There are, rightly, concerns about the ethics of involving children in research. 'Ethics' in the field of social research refers to principles that govern rules of conduct of researchers that are aimed at preventing subjects coming to any harm as a result of their involvement in the research.

Discussions about the particular ethical dilemmas posed for children as research subjects are at the forefront of the thinking of those who occupy the role of gatekeepers in access to research groups, but as yet there are only a few publications focusing specifically on the ethics of social research with children (see for example Alderson, 1995). This would tend to support my own experience, namely that those researchers who wish to involve children in their work are entering largely uncharted waters when trying to persuade gatekeepers that their own study is ethically sound. There do not appear to be yet in place procedures for ensuring that recognised ethical standards can be considered systematically alongside proposals for research with the result that the process of gaining the necessary permissions is fraught with difficulties and delays. Many researchers are forced to take a pragmatic approach and abandon plans to involve children directly in their studies. One such recent example concerns a study commissioned by the Department of Health to look at the use of expert witnesses in public law proceedings. The researchers were unable to obtain the necessary permissions to ask children about their experiences of being interviewed and assessed by experts within a time frame appropriate to the study, and thus the researchers have had to rely on the views of professionals, parents, and experts themselves, without the benefit of the children's contributions. This study when published is likely to be extremely influential in determining the ways in which experts are used in the future and yet, one of the main consumers of this service, children involved in public law proceedings, have been effectively denied any input into the process through their exclusion from one of its importance.

This chapter aims to explore some of the reasons that might account for the apparent reluctance on the part of gatekeepers to empower children to have a say in matters that concern them through an examination of two underlying value positions that are often in conflict: the protectionist and the liberationist. These are themes which emerged from empirical work undertaken in relation to a study aimed at eliciting children's perceptions of the *Guardian ad litem* service, in an attempt to understand the nature of the reluctance to allow children the opportunity to contribute to our knowledge through their involvement in research. *Guardians ad litem* are a professional body set up primarily to ensure that children's interests are safeguarded in care and related proceedings, (Children Act 1989, section 41). Guardians are under a duty to ascertain and report on the child's wishes and feelings to the court in addition to making their own professional recommendation as to the outcome of proceedings, having regard to the principle of the paramountcy of the child's welfare. Protectionism, in the sense in which it is used here, refers to a value system that holds children as incompetent to make decisions about matters which concern them without guidance and involvement from adults on the grounds of their perceived immaturity and lack of experience, whilst in contrast, liberationism holds to the principle of expanded autonomy for children in line with their developing competence. It is proposed that the protectionist position is that most often adopted by those who occupy the powerful position of gatekeeper in the granting of access to this research population, even though this same group may at other times be firmly in the liberationist camp in their own professional involvement with children. It is further suggested that adopting a protectionist position affords some measure of protection for the gatekeepers themselves, whilst recognising that they have an important function to fulfil in preventing the exploitation of vulnerable subjects for the purposes of research, or the advancement of the researcher's career. Analysing and understanding the nature of, and hence the necessity for, the protectionist stance adopted by gatekeepers may provide the researcher with the key to unlocking the door that often prevents access to this research population.

The *Children's Perceptions of their Guardians ad Litem's* study.
The following account of the *'Children's Perceptions'* study will be used to highlight the difficulties facing researchers who have to work alongside those with whom they do not share a value base, or with professionals whose own value systems are in conflict as a result of the threats posed to them by the potential outcome of the research. Through exploring ways in which difficulties were overcome it is intended that others considering embarking on research which empowers children and other vulnerable groups to contribute to knowledge, may be helped to avoid the obstacles that come between the researcher and those she wishes to learn from. Further, it is important to recognise that research can potentially be harmful to subjects as well as helpful. If the researcher understands the different ways in which those who have control over access seek to fulfil their responsibilities, then anticipation of the hurdles to be overcome may lead to the development of a more ethically and methodologically sound proposal, which in turn will involve fewer obstacles to overcome in the process of gaining permission. I shall begin by describing the context of the study in some detail in order to give the reader the opportunity to fully explore the dilemmas posed by this particular study for those charged with the responsibility of giving or withholding their permission to invite children to consider participating in this research. I shall then go on to examine the processes involved in obtaining the necessary permissions to conduct a study of children's perceptions of the consultative processes that operate in

legal proceedings which concern them. Finally, I shall explore some of the reasons that might explain the difficulties encountered and will give consideration to ways in which researchers might anticipate and develop strategies for advancing their research aims.

Much current UK legislation relating to children emphasises the importance of consulting them, and courts are required to have regard to the wishes and feelings of children, considered in the light of their age and understanding. Since May 1985 *Guardians ad litem* are the main professional body that has been charged with responsibility for representing children's interests and views in certain legal proceedings, and conveying these to the courts. These are known as public law proceedings and they are largely concerned with situations in which the State wishes to assume powers to make decisions about children that normally would only be taken by their parents. These decisions involve matters such as where the child should live, whom he should see and how often, what schools he should attend, and the nature of the arrangements that are made for his daily care. In order to obtain the court's authority to interfere in what would normally be considered to be private family business, the State must demonstrate that the child has suffered, or is likely to suffer, significant harm and that this is attributable to the care he receives from his parents.

Guardians ad litem are social workers who have particular expertise and lengthy experience of working with children and families, and they are regarded by the courts as experts in their field. Courts rely heavily on the advice and recommendations of the guardian who, in addition to reporting to the court the wishes and views of children, is required to give her own view as to what is in their best interests. The guardian is acknowledged as having considerable power to influence the outcome of proceedings.

The study discussed here arose out of curiosity about the manner in which guardians balance children's rights to have their wishes respected, and their rights to have their best interests protected. Its purpose was to enquire whether children as consumers of the guardian service believe that their views have been sought, respected, and relayed to the court, and to identify any aspects of practice that might influence the extent to which children are satisfied or otherwise with the service they receive. Furthermore, this study was intended to provide information to guardians that would assist them in assessing to what extent they meet their own aims and objectives in providing a service to young people and to empower children to contribute to the professional development of those charged with the statutory duty of eliciting and representing their views in care and related proceedings.

Ethical considerations

The study itself aimed to reflect a model of good practice in consultancy through consideration of the special needs of children as research subjects. Children can experience their *guardian ad litem* as a powerful and influential person who may in the future act again as their guardian and as such need reassurance in regard to confidentiality. Children themselves, in addition to those who have responsibility for them, were provided with information about the purpose and nature of this research. Informed agreement to participate was required of both the child and those with parental responsibility for him.

Children's parents, their carers, and their social workers where the local authority had parental responsibility for the child were consulted, provided with information about the study, and, where appropriate, their permission was sought before the child was contacted. Consultation prior to contacting children was aimed at ensuring that any child who it was thought would be distressed or unduly upset as a result of being invited to participate in the study would not be contacted. It was considered possible that some of the children who did agree to be interviewed may become distressed as a result of the interview itself bringing back painful memories, and contingency plans were in place to deal with this situation. The principle of the paramountcy of the child's welfare being as important in research as in the exercise of the guardian's duties was given due recognition in that the methodology reflected the belief that working in partnership with others involved in a child's life is crucial if the child's welfare is to be safeguarded, and in acceptance of the fact that some children would prefer not to participate in the study. It had to be recognised that providing opportunities that allow for people to decline to be involved in or to withdraw from the study would result in an element of self-selection, rather than the ideal of a sequentially gathered group. It is further recognised that the process of seeking the opinions of professionals, parents, and/or carers, whilst necessary to avoid undue distress for some vulnerable children, may have allowed those who feared exposing themselves to criticism from the child to deny those children the opportunity of deciding whether to participate in the study, thereby resulting in a distortion of the sample. This is most likely to have arisen in situations where children and their guardians ad litem were in conflict with the child's parents, their carers, or their social workers.

The process of gaining permissions for access to the research population

On reflection it seems that I entered this arena with certain assumptions which were not to prove helpful to my aim: that of gaining access to the research population. These assumptions can be summarised as follows:

- That everyone is interested, and stands to gain from the pursuit of knowledge

- That research cannot be 'harmful' if properly conducted
- Organisations with authority will rubber stamp applications if the methodology is sound
- Government departments share common ideologies
- That gatekeepers will engage in discussion with researchers on the basis of mutual respect.

The many different groups who had to be consulted, some of which had the power to refuse permission for access to the research population, others who did not have this formal power but could none the less exert great influence on those who did, can be divided under four main headings: local organisations, external authorities, parents and others with parental responsibility, and children. I shall now describe the nature of the difficulties that arose, some of which can, with the benefit of hindsight, be directly related to these inaccurate assumptions. The ways of overcoming the difficulties encountered will be identified in the hope that others can benefit from the lessons learnt in the process of obtaining access to this research population.

Local organisations
The key local organisations with whom it was necessary to consult were the manager of the guardians ad litem, the management committee for the Panel of Guardians ad Litem, and the guardians on the panel. It was necessary to have the support of the manager for the Panel of Guardians ad Litem, and that of the Panel management committee to which the manager is responsible, as it was only through the panel administrative system that I could gain access to the data base for the sample. It was also necessary to have the approval of the Director of Social Services as the management committee reports to the Director, and additionally, his permission is required to interview children on care orders for whom the local authority have parental responsibility.

The manager of the Panel of Guardians ad Litem was supportive of this study from the outset, and, given her influence with the management committee and within the local authority, it was relatively easy to gain the approval of both the committee and the Director of Social Services. However, the fact that this study did not pose any threat in terms of its outcome for either group was probably a more influential factor. Indeed, the panel manager, and in turn the management committee, saw advantages in the research in that the outcome, although this was not intended, could be viewed as a measure of quality control for the service.

Some guardians on the panel however initially took a different view and they saw that potential disadvantages for themselves could result from the data collected from their child clients. Guardians were, rightly and understandably, sensitive to the fact that it was their 'quality' which was being measured in the process of collecting data on children's views of the service they provide. Given that the very essence of the guardian's role is to elicit and represent the views of children, it would have been incongruent for this professional group to argue that children's views on the service were of no interest. Some guardians, who for the most part in their professional lives can be said to adopt a libertarian stance in that they typically facilitate the expression of children's views, adopted a protectionist position in regard to the issue of children's involvement in the proposed research. Objections were raised on the grounds that these vulnerable children needed to be 'protected' from the distress that could be associated with interviewing them for the purposes of research; that this group had already been subjected to many interviews and that therefore it would not be in their interests to expose them to a further interview; and that it would be potentially harmful to the children to ask them to comment on their experience of having a *guardian ad litem* given that guardians are seen as powerful people – hence children who commented negatively might be anxious about the implications of so doing.

In that this study was entirely congruent with the *raison d'être* of the *guardian ad litem* service I had confidently expected that guardians as a professional body would fully support the aims and objectives of this research. I had not anticipated that, in the face of a perceived threat, some individuals would adopt a protectionist position in contrast to the views that are more commonly expressed by this professional body, that children should be empowered and given a voice. Some guardians argued that to involve children in research by asking them directly about their experiences of the *Guardian ad Litem Service* would be potentially damaging and they put forward a case for children being protected from the dangers inherent in research, for example the sensationalised and misleading reporting of results.

Before being able to engage the support of guardians I had to take into account their needs to be protected as individuals from the potential harm that could occur to them as a result of this research if the children interviewed were to make negative comments about their individual performance. The measures taken included informing guardians, and children, that any comments made, whether positive or negative, would not be relayed by the researcher to the guardian concerned, or anyone else. It was particularly important for guardians to be given reassurances that the research would not become a quality assurance measure of any individual's practice and that confidentiality would be respected. The only exception to this would be if a child indicated that he or she had been harmed. In practice this has often turned out to be a source of frustration as I would so much like to tell guardians about the many wonderful things children have told me about them but, clearly, I cannot as this guarantee of confidentiality is the only way of protecting both children and guardians from their very real fears that the research process itself may be harmful to individuals. When guardians were reassured as to their own protection most felt able to give their support to the involvement of children in this study. It is of interest to note that when it was proposed that a second *guardian ad litem* panel be involved in a mirror study, the support for the study was unanimous amongst guardians from the outset. The measures described above that were taken to protect guardians were by that time already in place and it seems likely that it was this that was an influential factor in preventing this second group of guardians from adopting a protectionist position in relation to what was essentially the same research proposal that had been presented to the first panel.

External organisations

The Department of Health is responsible for the administration of the *Guardian ad Litem Service* and as such it was important to inform those concerned of the proposal to conduct a study on children's perceptions of the service from the outset, and to seek their advice and comments at every stage of the design process. Historically the Department of Health as an organisation has a strong commitment to innovative research, and much interest and support were expressed at the idea of directly involving children in attempts to learn more about the *Guardian ad Litem Service*. In addition, the quality control aspect of the research had similar appeal for the department responsible for the administration of the service as it did for the panel management committees responsible for local administration.

In addition to gaining the informal approval and support of the Department of Health, it was necessary to have the formal agreement of the *Lord Chancellor's Department*. The Lord Chancellor's Department has responsibility for authorising research relating to court matters where access to court records, court personnel, or people who are the responsibility of the court is required. A particular problem in negotiating with this department revolved around the apparent absence of any formal guidelines for researchers to assist them in supplying the information required by those who have the responsibility for approving proposals. As methodology and supportive documentation had been thoroughly scrutinised by experienced academic researchers and had the support of the

Department of Health, the Panel Manager, the management committee and the Director of Social Services, it was with confidence and anticipation of beginning to collect data that I awaited the rubber stamp of the Lord Chancellor's Department. I had however failed to consider the manner in which the Lord Chancellor's Department might be adversely affected by this research.

The responsibility for giving or withholding consent to undertaking research with vulnerable groups brings with it the duty to ensure that those affected by it will come to no harm. It is clear that children can be at risk of exploitation from research and that the needs of the researcher and/or the agency commissioning the research may be in conflict with those of the children they wish to study. The Lord Chancellor's Department in common with other gatekeepers were, and rightly so, anxious to ensure that this research proposal was sensitive to the needs of children to be protected from both potentially damaging aspects of the process of being involved in research and that the information obtained was likely to be of benefit to this group. They were further concerned to ensure that, should problems arise, no blame could be attached to the Lord Chancellor or his staff. Unlike the staff at the Department of Health, the Panel Manager, the *Guardians ad Litem Service,* and the Panel management committee, the Lord Chancellor's staff had no previous knowledge of my work or those who could comment on it, and hence nothing upon which to base any confidence in my competence for the task. The Lord Chancellor's Department adopted a strongly protectionist position and it was only as a result of the process of engaging in much discussion over some 16 months about the respective merits of different methodologies, the ethical dilemmas of engaging children of different ages in research, the practical administrative details involved in the collection of data, and my willingness to compromise on some matters, that those responsible felt they had properly satisfied themselves. This rigorous examination of every aspect of my thinking was, with hindsight, a valuable experience although the process was made unnecessarily painful as a result of there being no clear structures or time limits within which we were all operating, and that the staff responsible were neither familiar with methodological and ethical aspects of research nor with children as a client group. Whilst this led to those concerned asking questions that might well have been posed by the uninformed but responsible 'man in the street' who (it is proposed) could be expected to adopt a protectionist position and have little knowledge of alternative approaches to issues of children's rights and needs (and this was in itself at times constructive and enlightening), it also led to difficulties in establishing effective and mean-ingful communication. This aspect of the work of the Lord Chancellor's Department is low priority in relation to almost everything else with the result that written communications and phone calls were often not responded to, and meetings of all those involved were difficult to arrange. It does seem that the internal structures operating within the Lord Chancellor's Department in relation to the granting of permission to undertake research, would benefit from urgent review if children are to be able to contribute to ethically and methodologically sound studies. In the meantime, in order to ensure that matters progress at all, the would-be researcher must be prepared to be proactive if their work is not to be buried and forgotten, and to build into their studies timescales that allow considerable margins for delay.

Parents, and others with parental responsibility

Having finally obtained the consent and approval of all the professional bodies, my next hurdle was to convince parents, carers, and social workers responsible for those children who were on care orders, to allow me access to the children. The lessons learnt thus far led me to ensure that the literature developed for these groups addressed the concerns likely to be uppermost in their minds.

Although the study was conceived to learn about children's views of the service I decided at a very late stage to include parents' views, largely on the basis that if parents themselves were involved in the study this would likely facilitate access. Only two parents were unwilling for themselves and their children to be included in the sample. Those who did participate expressed appreciation that their views were considered to be of interest. It is interesting to note that none of the parents raised any concerns about the risks posed to their children by being interviewed by researchers, notwithstanding their unanimous view that the experience of being involved in court proceedings was difficult and highly stressful for all concerned.

Social workers have been similarly supportive of children's inclusion in this study and in only three cases did consultation with workers result in a decision not to invite a child to participate, for reasons of sensitivity in the cases at that time. Individual social workers were not likely to be threatened by the outcome of this research and the majority were prepared to give generously of their time in arranging access between the children and researcher. That this is in stark contrast to the initial response of guardians to the study would seem to lend support to the contention that underlying their intellectual objections lay the perceived threat to the professional group.

Children

Only one child invited to participate has so far declined to be included in the study. My own experience confirms that of other researchers referred to earlier;

namely, that children feel empowered by inclusion in research which seeks their opinions about matters that affect them and actively welcome the opportunity to state their views. The experience has shown that they have a valid and extremely important contribution to make as a result of their personal experiences of the *Guardian ad Litem Service*.

Suggestions for researchers wishing to access vulnerable research populations

Researchers need to bear in mind that their relationship with those who have both formal and informal control of access to research subjects is one of unequal power, that their respective value positions may be in conflict, and that research generally, and their individual study in particular, may pose hidden and unacknowledged threats for groups and individuals. It may prove helpful to give consideration to the ways in which 'the gatekeepers' might be affected by the outcome of the proposed study. Any possible advantages to their participation should be highlighted in discussions and written communications. Attention should be paid to the different measures that could be built into the methodology with the aim of allaying their worst fears and addressing their concerns. In this regard it may benefit the researcher to consider whether the 'gatekeepers' adopt a protectionist or liberationist perspective in their thinking about the group to which one wants access, and if so how this can be taken into account in the context of written and verbal communications. It may be beneficial to consider whether there are enticements that could be offered, for example advance notice of, or opportunity to comment on, publications arising from the study. In negotiating access the researcher may have to consider whether there is a place for pragmatism. In what areas might the researcher envisage reaching a compromise between his or her ideals and those of the gatekeepers?

The importance of personal contacts is difficult to overestimate. Where the researcher is unknown to gatekeepers, particularly those that are operating in protectionist mode, the involvement of others who are known and respected by them is likely to allay some of their fears and thus assist in the process of gaining their confidence and support. This is as true when dealing with remote government officials as it is when attempting to engage the interest of those closest to the research subject, as borne out by my own experience of having the support of social workers known to the parents and children invited to participate in the study. This, together with appropriate attention in the methodology being directed towards the reality of the likely fears and concerns of the gatekeepers, will assist in allaying fears and concerns.

Perhaps most important of all is to view the gatekeepers as partners in the sense that we all have a collective responsibility to ensure that research involving vulnerable individuals is respectful of their needs. One needs to listen carefully and take account of the whole spectrum of views expressed. It is better to anticipate that compromise will be necessary rather than assume that certain academic and/or professional groups will have the definitive solutions to the ethical dilemmas facing those wishing to empower vulnerable groups to participate in research aimed at the acquisition of knowledge about them.

Conclusion

It appears that researchers, and those who use the knowledge obtained through research, are beginning to recognise the importance of the contributions that children and other dependent groups can make to our knowledge and understanding. This looks set to become an exciting and developing field, and one in which many challenges lie ahead. We need to develop sensitive approaches to both research populations and gatekeepers if we are to overcome the considerable hurdles that at present make it difficult, but not impossible, to involve vulnerable groups in the acquisition of knowledge about them and their needs, and to allow them to contribute to the professional development of those who are charged with the responsibility of providing services for them. It is hoped that this account of what has been a most rewarding and interesting journey, despite, or perhaps because of, its frustrations and challenges, will assist others contemplating similar endeavours, and that it might encourage those who had not thought of doing so to involve vulnerable groups directly in their studies.

References

Alderson, P. (1993). *Children's Consent to Surgery*. Open University Press.

Alderson, P. (1995). *Listening to Children: Children, Ethics and Social Research*. Barnardos.

Department of Health (1990). *Principles and Practice in Regulation and Guidance*. London: HMSO.

Department of Health (1995). *Messages From Research*. London: HMSO

Mayall, B. ed. (1994). *Children's Childhoods: Observed and Experienced*. London: Falmer Press.

Morrow and Richards (1996). The Ethics of Social Research with Children: An Overview. *Children And Society* (10) pp90-105.

Sharland, E., Jones, D., Aldgate, J., Seal, H. and Croucher, M. (1995). *Professional Intervention in Child Sexual Abuse*. HMSO.

Part Two

Research contexts, concepts and contracts

Chapter 7
Social work research, social work knowledge and the research assessment exercise

Mike Fisher

Introduction

Social work research is conducted in many settings in the UK, including agencies, as part of DipSW qualifying programmes, and universities. This chapter is about the way social work research is conducted in universities, as this is by far the largest body of social work research, and one which is publicly supported by research funds allocated by the Higher Education Funding Councils (HEFC). It is also the body of research which is under the greatest scrutiny: as part of university research, social work is evaluated during the periodic Research Assessment Exercises (RAE).

The RAE was conducted by the Higher Education Funding Councils in 1986, 1989, 1992, and 1996, and applies to all academic disciplines. The principle of peer review is used to assess the quality of work of academics submitted by universities in particular disciplines. The outcome is a research rating on what was in 1996 effectively a seven point scale for each discipline, which forms part of a funding formula used to allocate funds to universities. As universities compete to be seen as research leaders and attempt to solidify their funding base following the enormous, and only partly funded, expansion of student numbers in the last 10 years there is increasing emphasis on the RAE performance as the core performance indicator.

The principle is that research funds should be targeted on areas of excellence, both to demonstrate accountability for the use of public funds and to encourage further research growth around existing excellence. The best example of this is the decision following the 1996 RAE that research funds would be restricted to those disciplines scoring three or above on the scale. Universities and departments where research of a lower quality rating was undertaken would have to find other ways of supporting their work than through HEFC research funds.

This chapter will examine the nature of social work knowledge and research, and question the underlying principle of selectivity as it applies to social work research conducted in universities. The effects on the nature and value of social work research will be explored, in order to assess whether this research addresses the knowledge needs of policy makers and practitioners in social care.

Identifying social work knowledge and research

Social work research is often hard to identify, and in academic circles greater credit may accrue through designating the research as part of social policy and administration. Certainly, in the 1992 RAE, key areas of research relevant to social work were submitted under the discipline of social policy (such as the work of the Dartington Social Research Unit on child care) or even under town and country planning (such as the work of what was then the School of Advanced Urban Studies at the University of Bristol on community care). The work of the Dartington Social Research Unit demonstrates the concealed nature of much investigation relevant to social work research. There is no doubt that the Unit's 1986 research on children (*Lost in Care* Millham *et al.*, 1986) played a leading role in revealing the shortcomings in the public care of children, and contributed to the reform of legislation under the Children Act 1989. It was summarised in the 1986 DHSS Research Review *Social Work Decisions in Child Care*, and became one of the key references in the teaching of child care social work and in research on public care. Despite its relevance to social work research, the work of the Unit was returned in the 1992 RAE under the academic discipline of social policy. In contrast, my own research with colleagues *In and Out of Care*, also one of the nine key studies summarised in *Social Work Decisions in Child Care*, was returned under the academic discipline of social work (Fisher, Marsh and Phillips, 1986). The rationale for these decisions lay in the academic structures of the two universities concerned, particularly in the history of social policy within those universities, rather than in any decision about the fundamental subject discipline.

Something of this confusion is visible in the department location of social work as a university discipline. Often the index of university departments requires some intensive research to reveal the presence of social work in departments or schools of social policy, applied social studies, applied social sciences, social and administrative studies, policy studies, human relations or even sociological studies. For example, the work of Eric Sainsbury at the University of Sheffield, which laid much of the foundation for the current emergence of the users' voice in social work (Sainsbury, 1975; Sainsbury, Nixon and Phillips, 1982), was undertaken in a department of sociological studies, which houses sociology, social policy, and social work. This confusion may also extend to academic leadership. Many of the leading figures in social work research in the UK do not have social work in their professorial title, and some universities with social work have no professorial leadership. There is thus no clear identity for social work, either in the bricks and mortar of universities or in the people who profess it.

At the root of this is the problem whether social work is 'really' an academic discipline. Although social work is sometimes compared with health subjects or with sociology, the comparison is usually drawn with social policy, which has a longer academic history in universities, and a more established public profile. There are many possible explanations for university scepticism about the academic status of social work, but one key issue is the contrast between the focus in universities on *subjects*, single disciplines, rooted in an exclusive knowledge base, and the focus in the applied field on *bodies of knowledge*, which have roots in many different disciplines and whose distinguishing characteristic is that they are relevant in practice. For much of their history, universities have pursued knowledge in the form of discrete disciplines, with defined (if sometimes indefensible) boundaries. In the latter half of the twentieth century, however, the greater integration of university-based knowledge with economic activity has led to a demand for knowledge that works, or for applied knowledge with practical relevance, and this kind of knowledge frequently crosses what were once heavily patrolled boundaries.

In social work, for example, we have seen how anthropology and philosophy have infused the study of mental health and mental illness with an appreciation of the social context and meaning of behaviour (Bateson, Barthes, Foucault). Similarly, communication theorists have brought new understandings to the studies of families, and much of what used to be called crime or illness is now studied with the benefit of the sociology of deviance. The fact that this kind of knowledge is interdisciplinary may be so obvious to today's reader that the transition from single *subjects* is no longer visible. To those working in the social sciences during the sixties and seventies, however, there was no doubting the emergence of a wide range of new bodies of knowledge, whose distinguishing factor was that they did not belong to any single one of the traditional disciplines. The popularity of Pearson's *The Deviant Imagination: Psychiatry, Social Work and Social Change* (1975), arose from the way it crystallized how social processes could be better studied when scholars are free to cross traditional subject boundaries. Instead of studying within a subject discipline, academics were free to place social processes at the centre of study, and to draw on whatever branches of knowledge helped to promote understanding and relevant intervention.

The knowledge base of social work is thus diffuse, diverse, and inclusive. It places the issue, problem or person at the centre of investigation and tries to understand events through available knowledge. Placing the client, user, issue or problem at the centre of activity is what Philp calls 'creating the subject', meaning that, for example, someone who offends is not defined exclusively or primarily in terms of the offence, but as a person in a social context within which the offence occurred (Philp, 1979). Legal, medical or psychiatric explanations tend to atomise the individual, whose behaviour is better understood in the context of an interplay of different social science perspectives, unified in the vision of the social worker.

This conception of social work might seem remote from the practicalities of everyday practice, but it is primarily because we are dissecting it that the processes seem complex. In fact, most social workers go about their daily business untroubled by the need to create a 'subject' in Philp's terms, or by the need consciously to synthesize material from different knowledge bases, simply because it is what they are educated and trained to do and because they often do it rather well. This helps to explain why conventional thinking about social workers' use of knowledge (often specified as 'theory') suggests that they do not use it much because they do not report its use (see, for example, Carew, 1979). Carew mistakes a low ability to verbalise knowledge in practice as a low ability to use it. Similar thinking lies behind the often repeated call for greater use of research in practice and for greater emphasis on evidence-based practice (Department of Health, 1994), neither of which appears to be underpinned by concerted and systematic enquiry into either the kind of knowledge required for practice or the extent of research in use by practitioners.

None of this is, of course, to argue that all is well with social work as a discipline, or to argue against improving the use of knowledge or research in practice: rather the question is that the kind of knowledge required for practice has not been sufficiently examined, and is almost certainly neither the propositional knowledge of the social sciences nor the rather restricted categories of knowledge suggested by proponents of evidence-based practice (for a partial review, see Fisher, 1998). Clearly it would be preferable if practitioners had the ability to name their knowledge and reflect on its use, since this would give them and their public greater confidence in their expertise and would considerably facilitate their professional development (Eraut, 1994; Schön, 1995). However, if social work knowledge is knowledge-in-action as much as knowledge-for-understanding, and if knowledge-in-action is necessarily inconspicuous (so that practitioners can get on and act) it should not be surprising that its practitioners sometimes find it difficult to explicate.

The net result is that social work as a discipline properly belongs to the new range of knowledge bases required for modern understanding of social issues. The key question is whether social work appropriately integrates knowledge from a wide field of social science (including its own) and productively brings it to bear on social issues. This is a serious question for social work to answer, and it is not my assertion that social work has by any means a clean bill of health. My point is that this is not the same question as is conventionally posed when the issue of whether social work is 'really' an academic discipline arises. Indeed, the principal question conventionally posed – whether social work creates its own, exclusive knowledge base – and which is usually answered in the negative (see, for example, Sibeon, 1990) is not only wrong in terms of its misunderstanding of the nature of social work knowledge, but downright anachronistic in terms of the interdisciplinary social science approach to understanding modern social issues. Social work knowledge, like all modern knowledge, must be inclusive of a range of perspectives, and not exclusively tied to single subject disciplines.

This confusion surrounding the academic place of social work is further reflected in the funding of social work research. Research relevant to social work is sometimes publicly supported by government, in the shape of studies commissioned by the Department of Health Research and Development Division, and by research foundations, such as the Joseph Rowntree Foundation. This support is rarely, however, directed specifically at developing social work research. For example, the work on the education and training of social workers (Marsh and Triseliotis, 1996) was primarily commissioned to answer questions about the social work workforce. Major research units, such as the Personal Social Services Research Unit at the University of Kent at Canterbury, the Dartington Social Research Unit at the University of Bristol, and the Research Unit at the National Institute for Social Work are funded by the DoH to undertake programmes of policy-relevant research required by government. Although these programmes are often directly relevant to the practice of social work, they are not funded specifically to progress social work as an academic discipline, and their benefits to the discipline are more a by-product than a deliberate strategy. It is arguable that the only UK research unit specifically exploring social work as a research discipline is the Social Work Research Centre at the University of Stirling. The Centre for Evidence-based Social Services at the University of Exeter, funded for three years as a regional experiment by DoH and by participating local authorities, again has a brief in which research relevant to social work will certainly be undertaken, but which, as its title suggests, is as equally focused on social services as on social work as a discipline.

One of the major sources of social science research support in the UK, the ESRC, does not explicitly support social work research, as it does not recognize it as a discipline. Research such as Lewis and Glennerster's study of the implementation of community care, part of which directly examines the implementation of a new form of social work practice, care management, was funded by the ESRC as social policy research (Lewis and Glennerster, 1996). There is of course nothing untoward in this: my point is merely that the study contains research directly relevant to social work as a discipline, which the funding process does not (and in the case of the ESRC, cannot) make visible.

This brief review of the nature of social work research and knowledge and its position in UK universities has concentrated on conceptual issues. Space is too short to examine in detail such important, but predominantly practical, questions as the lack of a traditional career track into academic social work, the breadth of responsibilities of social work academics, the repeated reorganisations of social work education required by CCETSW, and the impact of the government decision not to extend social work education and training programmes to a minimum of three years in line with the broad picture in Europe. Although different from the conceptual issues, all these factors nevertheless constrain academic social work.

The criteria for assessment under the RAE
Although the principle of peer review remains constant, the conduct of each RAE is slightly different. The assessment covers the number of research staff, published work, postgraduate studentships, research plans, and research income. The most problematic issues are which staff are selected and how quality is determined. The 1992 exercise required universities to select staff deemed to be 'actively undertaking research', and to select their two 'best' research articles and books and up to 'two other forms of public output'. The assessment panels also received information on the total number of articles or books published as a 'volume' measure. A five point scale was used, ranging from a '5', where some work was of international excellence and the rest of national excellence, to a '1', where none or virtually none of the work was of national excellence. The 1996 exercise altered the requirements so that four pieces of published work were selected, and the rating scale was extended by the addition of a starred '5' and a subdivided '3', making it effectively a seven point scale (see Appendix 1). Although panels again received information on the volume of public output, it was not intended that this would be part of the assessment of quality.

These arrangements have several implications for the assessment of social work. First, the organisational confusion in universities about the location and leadership of social work meant that decisions about which staff were active were often not based in a clear understanding of social work as a discipline.

If social work was a minor part of a social science grouping, and if leadership rested with academics from another discipline, it was difficult to see how an expert internal assessment of the strengths and weaknesses of social work could be undertaken. Thus the designation of the body of researchers active in social work, and the agenda for research development often lay outside the hands of social work academics. The reverse — where the designation of non-social work academics as research active lay in the hands of social work academics — rarely applied in UK universities. In his review of the 1996 RAE and Social Policy, Craig also suggests that social policy may have suffered through being subsumed under other social science disciplines (1997).

A joint assessment panel was established to cover both social policy and social work. This might be seen as recognition of shared territory between the two disciplines, or as inability to grasp the nettle of distinguishing them. The published account veers towards the former explanation, claiming that separate panels would have led to 'rather artificial divisions of the subject matter between social policy and social work' (Cheetham and Deakin, 1997: 436). Later in the account, however, we read of the panel's surprise that social work research lacked 'examination of the implications of increasing child and family poverty' (p.440) and it was pointed out that this kind of research *was* present in social policy research. This statement ignores the politics of the RAE. Decisions were taken by submitting universities about the disciplinary designation of research on the implications of child and family poverty, and the outcome that it was submitted as social policy deserves some critical analysis. Since the same account also raised questions about the 'wide range of topics addressed under the "social policy" rubric' (original quotes) and reported that the boundaries of the subject had been expanded (p.440), one obvious avenue of enquiry is whether this expansion might have led to an overlap with related disciplines.

This does not necessarily mean any impropriety in the designation of research as social work or social policy. My point is that the 1996 RAE required work relevant to both disciplines to be submitted under one only, and that existing power structures in UK universities are more likely to lead to the designation of any work which can be brought into a relationship with social policy as social policy research, than they are to lead to the ascription of social policy research relevant to social work as social work research.

The general definition of the different levels for quality ratings was set by the HEFCs to apply to all disciplines, and the assessment of research quality increases with the greater national and international recognition in the greater number of areas (Appendix 1). In addition, each panel created its own public statement of criteria for excellence. In the case of the Social Policy and Social Work Panel, the criteria emphasized the inappropriateness of a formal hierarchy of publications, a recognition of links with what were called 'user communities', and of the different circumstances in different parts of the UK.

On the face of it, these criteria usefully recognized some of the constraints for social work as a discipline. In particular, the relatively restricted opportunities for academic journal publication in social work would have disadvantaged the discipline if a simple hierarchy of journals had been created with the quality of the work equated with the quality of the journal. Social work submissions typically contain academics with at least some of their four 'best' publications in the form of reports for funding agencies or sponsoring groups. Such work is not normally generously funded, and commissioners do not always want their research time used to explore the national, let alone international, implications — one of the key elements in the general criteria used to judge excellence.

The question about the place of locally or nationally commissioned work also connects with the role of 'user communities' in evaluating the impact of research. The Social Policy and Social Work Panel described this as a 'complex remit' and the term as 'ugly and misleading'. The Panel met with what it called 'the consultative users group' and reported that the discussion, though 'pitched at a general level', was helpful in 'clarifying user perspectives'. No further meetings were held. This left unclear whether the Panel accepted that service users were included in 'user communities', and if so what weight was attached to their views. The list of groups invited to the user group consultation included 'community groups', but no details are given. This stands in contrast with the development of emancipatory models of research in social care (Beresford and Wallcroft, 1997; Evans and Fisher, 1998a; Evans and Fisher, 1998b), which suggest that social work researchers should seek to involve service users in the design and conduct of the research, and should regard service users as a key audience for their dissemination. A submission to the HEFCE by the SWRA suggested

> there should be explicit acknowledgement of service users of social welfare agencies as one of the 'user communities'. This would correspond to the emphasis the Association gives to collaboration with service users in practice research, and would increase the scope for recognizing the different methods of public 'output' relevant to service users (SWRA, 1995).

As this note makes clear, the issue is not just that service users should be seen as part of the 'user community', it is also that dissemination to the service user community should be a high priority for social work researchers. This kind of dissemination is time consuming, and relies more on personal contact and carefully prepared briefings than on learned works. A similar argument applies to some elements of the manager and practitioner audience, for whom formal academic papers or book-length work may be inaccessible and inappropriate. Much of the dissemination to service user and manager and practitioner audiences will more often be local, than either national or international, and will have more impact than the often-long-delayed formal publications. The energy and commitment of researchers in dissemination to both service user and manager and practitioner audiences deserve, therefore, greater recognition in research assessment, as does the creation of brief, accessible reference material for both audiences. Without such recognition, it appears that the Social Policy and Social Work Panel gave greater weight to material which social work researchers wrote for each other.

The Social Policy and Social Work Panel also emphasized its high regard for 'significant new theory or research' (RAE 96 3/95, para.4) or 'significant new theory and originality in content and methods of research (Cheetham and Deakin, 1997: 436). However, theory is a complex notion, and it would have been helpful to have had the Panel's understanding and the connection with originality explained. For example, the common distinction between formal and substantive theory (distinguishing between the application of an explanatory framework to broad social processes or to specific policy and practice issues) is critical to much social work research, which is driven more by policy and practice than by theoretical concerns. Both approaches are capable of yielding theoretical development, but it is a formal goal of the latter and a by-product of the former.

Policy and practice concerns dominate the funding of research. Most funding agencies look primarily for policy-relevant research which will throw light on social issues and explore potential solutions. For example, the single largest, non-governmental funder, the Joseph Rowntree Foundation, explicitly requires research with a developmental focus, aimed at exploring solutions not just at documenting problems. The DoH Research and Development Division has a formal brief to commission *policy-relevant* research. Neither, of course, objects to the presence of theoretical concerns in proposals, but their funding decisions are not primarily influenced by whether the research will further social theory. The ESRC, of course, is interested in funding work which explores social theory *per se*, but it does not recognize social work as a discipline.

There is thus no co-ordinated funding strategy designed to produce social work theory, let alone theory with greater applicability than the substantive kind.

Indeed, one of the pre-requisites of the move from substantive to formal theory is the existence of large bodies of research, focused on similar or overlapping areas of investigation, or indeed directly replicating earlier work, so that the theory can be tested in different circumstances and its robustness assessed. Strauss describes the process of 'elaborating an extant theory' as involving

> multiple and ultimately systematic comparisons of various conditional dimensions as we look then for various associated interactions, processes, strategies and consequences (Strauss, 1995: 16).

This kind of concerted enquiry is simply not available in the UK approach to social work research funding. Indeed, the fact that a study overlaps with a previous study may be taken by the funding body as a reason not to provide support. The emphasis on theory in the deliberations of the Social Policy and Social Work Panel requires critical analysis of the nature of theory for social work, and of the feasibility of different kinds of theory creation in the context of UK research-funding strategies.

A critical account of the 1996 RAE outcome for social work
The final question is whether the RAE has assisted or hindered the development of social work research. Parts of this question may be approached through quantitative analysis, and Appendix 2 reports the full tabulation of results for the UK in social work and social policy for 1992 and 1996. Social policy is included because I argued earlier that the subject designation is often a matter of historical bargaining, and it is likely that much research relevant to social work was submitted under social policy. An example of the reverse, where work relevant to social policy (and other disciplines) was returned under social work, may be seen in the only 5* social work rating, achieved by the Department of Applied Social Sciences at the University of Stirling, which houses the Social Work Research Centre. This table does not include all subjects relevant to social work research, since some will have been submitted under a health discipline or sociology (Lyons, 1997). Although there are complex issues in mapping the 1996 seven point scale onto the 1992 five point scale (see Craig, 1997), the approach taken here will be to equate the grades as far as possible, treating a 1996 '3b' as a 1992 '3'

Looking first at the universities submitting under social work for both RAEs, 20 achieved higher ratings in 1996 than in 1992, four maintained their existing rating, and one received a lower rating. Although it might be argued that this constitutes prima facie improvement, the 1996 assessment was undertaken with more transparency than that in 1992 (particularly in the publishing of panel assessment criteria) and most submissions were better constructed to give both the best account and the evidence sought for rating. In 1996, it was much clearer that the assessment included the quality of research management, both at the time of submission and into the future, and research plans gave this substantial emphasis. It might also be argued that the difference between a 1992 '3' and 1996 '3a' is extremely small, and that the three universities where this occurred should not be counted as having improved. The picture in social policy is similar in that 15 submissions received an improved rating, but 10 remained the same and none declined. Excluding those departments where a 1992 '3' became a 1996 '3a', 68% of social work submissions improved, compared with 52% of those in social policy. This does not necessarily mean that social work improved more than social policy, because there were more social policy submissions with higher ratings than social work submissions, with the result that the scope for improvement is reduced. A safer conclusion is that in both disciplines what improved was the quality of the submission.

In both disciplines, the 1996 RAE attracted new submissions: six in social work and 11 in social policy, often from so-called 'new' universities. However laudable their achievements, none in social work and only one in social policy achieved above a 3 rating. Although these universities may progress in the future, this suggests that (with one exception) the new submissions did not originate from universities which might *at the time of submission* be thought of as centres of research excellence.

One measure of absolute performance in 1996 (rather than relative improvement between the two RAEs) is to look at the proportion of those rated '4' or '5' (including 5*), departments the Social Policy and Social Work Panel termed 'highly rated'. The review by the Social Policy and Social Work Panel contains an acknowledged error in reporting that 'over two-thirds of social policy and one-third of social work submissions were rated 4 or 5' (Cheetham and Deakin, 1997: 437). The results over the UK as a whole are given in Table 1.

Table 1 Percentage of ratings by discipline 1996

Rating	Social Work		Social Policy	
	no.	%	no.	%
5 or 4	11	34	18	41
3	14	44	18	41
2 or 1	7	22	8	18

The raw picture is therefore that just over one third of social work submissions were rated '4' or '5', while the figure for social policy was just over two fifths. However, it remains true that there are 11 such centres in social work, but 18 in social policy. In terms of research-active staff, the 11 social work centres returned 153.6 staff (average 14) while the social policy centres returned 375.9 staff (average 21). Only one of the social work centres had a staff group above 20 (University of Stirling), while the figure for social policy is nine. The only '5*' centres in each discipline housed a national research unit, the Social Work Research Centre at the University of Stirling and the Personal Social Services Research Unit at LSE, suggesting that size of the academic staff group and continuity of funding play a role in creating research excellence.

The principle of the RAE is the selective redistribution of funds to augment existing excellence. Although the overall verdict of the 1996 RAE may be that it demonstrates improvement in social work as a discipline, it seems likely that we face the problems of insufficient critical mass or continuity in comparison with social policy. The question is how the principle of selectivity will affect the future of both these centres of social work research excellence and those which aspire to reach similar ratings in the next RAE.

Compared with their position in the 1992 RAE, units rated '4' or '5' in the 1996 had usually grown in terms of the number of research-active staff (Table 2).

Table 2:
Growth in research-active staff in units rated '4' or '5' in 1996 RAE

	1996	1992	% growth
Bristol	16.5	13.3	24.1
East Anglia	16.6	14.9	11.4
Huddersfield	11.0	6.9	59.4
Keele	14.0	10.4	34.6
Lancaster	12.8	9.0	42.2
Leicester	10.5	6.0	75.0
Warwick	10.6	10.0	6.0
York	15.6	9.0	73.3
Edinburgh	9.0	10.4	-13.5
Stirling	22.5	16.0	40.6
Wales, Swansea	14.5	10.0	45.0

With the exception of a small decrease in staff at the University of Edinburgh, all '4'- or '5'-rated units in 1996 had grown in relation to their 1992 size, some substantially. However, the single largest increase in research active staff was recorded by De Montfort University, whose 1996 return reported an increase from 4.8 to 12 (150%). Clearly, a simple increase in staff does not guarantee the achievement of a high quality rating, although it seems likely that the presence of larger numbers allows greater credibility in the designation of subgroups of research areas, and that this in turn suggests a managed research environment.

It is clearly possible that the '4'- and '5'-rated research centres in social work will continue to grow, and to absorb more of the UK resource of social work research staff. If this is a desired outcome of selective funding, we need to ask whether they are appropriately distributed as a national resource, and how to handle the less-highly-rated units. One obvious problem is that there is no '4' - or '5'-rated resource in the major centres of government in the England, Wales or Northern Ireland: Scotland has its resource appropriately located in Edinburgh. It is clearly illogical to allow selectivity to be the only principle, since it would eventually result in just one or two centres for each HEFC, regardless of concerns such as their geographical distribution. In taking account of national needs, we should also examine those research centres which achieved a '2' rating, meaning that up to half of the sub-areas of activity are of national relevance. This means that in seven universities (four of which were submitting in 1996 for the first time), nationally relevant research is not to be supported from HEFC research funds. The selectivity solution would be to move individual researchers rated as nationally relevant to '3'-, '4'- or '5'-rated units. This raises the problem of identifying them (since the Panel does not rate individual researchers) and of treating university staff as movable resources on the grounds of one of their professional activities.

If we are to preserve the *national* stock of *nationally* relevant research, some HEFC funds should be channelled towards maintaining research in '2'- rated units. Quite apart from any other considerations, the present system of selectivity means that no new university can enter the research assessment system unless it is able to predict with some certainty that a rating of '3' or above will be obtained, a leap made by just one university in social policy and by none in social work in 1996.

Conclusions
The RAE system of selective funding has radically changed the face of social work research in the UK. It has set a publishing agenda, which distorts some of the requirements of good dissemination and good relations with the field, and

created a two-tier academic staff group, where those deemed research-active are accorded the greater prestige. It ignores scholarship as part of teaching, and runs the risk of reducing the participation by leading social work researchers in the education of future social workers, and thus of future social work academics. This is reflected in the deeply ironic quote from the Dearing Committee, used in the 1997 consultation on the RAE, that 'some academic staff and departments were neglecting their academic activities in order to participate in the RAE' (RAE 97 2/97). Moreover, the current RAE is based on the outmoded concept of an exclusive discipline with a unique knowledge-base without appreciating the need for a different concept of social work knowledge, and it has favoured the development of theory without specifying what kind of theory is helpful or relevant to social work practice.

The cost of the 1996 RAE has been estimated at £28m. The Social Policy and Social Work Panel's review suggests an overall improvement in quality, yet the 1997-8 allocation of funds for social work research in England remained at the £2.7m it was in 1996-7, despite a 14% increase in the number of research staff in units rated '3' and above (HEFCE, 1997). In comparison with other academic disciplines with a health or social care practice focus, nursing research funding in England rose by 33%, funding for professionals allied to medicine by 26%, and funding for hospital-based clinical subjects by 18%. Funding for the most closely related university discipline, social policy, rose by 6%.

It seems clear from this analysis that the RAE is unlikely to deliver more funds to social work research, and that through selectivity alone it cannot supply nationally relevant resources for social work. It is time for social work as a discipline to lift its head above the local struggle for survival of individual research centres and to examine the cost to the discipline as a whole of the distortion by the RAE of the goals of the discipline.

Appendix 1 HEFC guidance on quality rating

5* Research quality that equates to attainable levels of international excellence in a majority of sub-areas of activity and attainable levels of national excellence in all others.

5 Research quality that equates to attainable levels of international excellence in some sub-areas of activity and to attainable levels of national excellence in virtually all others.

4 Research quality that equates to attainable levels of national excellence in virtually all sub-areas of activity, possibly showing some evidence of international excellence, or to international level in some, and at least national level in a majority.

3a Research quality that equates to attainable levels of national excellence in a substantial majority of the sub-areas of activity, or to international level in some, and to national level in others together constituting a majority.

3b Research quality that equates to attainable levels of national excellence in the majority of sub-areas of activity.

2 Research quality that equates to attainable levels of national excellence in up to half the sub-areas of activity.

1 Research quality that equates to attainable levels of national excellence in none, or virtually none, of the sub-areas of activity.

Appendix 2: RAE results in Social Policy and Social Work, UK, 1992 and 1996

	SOCIAL WORK		SOCIAL POLICY	
	1996	1992	1996	1992
Anglia Polytechnic	2	-		
Bath	3a	2	5	5
Birmingham	3a	3	4	4
Bradford	3a	3		
Brighton			3b	2
Bristol	4	3	5	3
Brunel College	3b	2	4	4
Buckinghamshire			3b	-
Cheltenham & Glos			2	-
De Montfort	2	1		
East Anglia	5	5		
Edge Hill			3b	-
Exeter	3b	2		
Goldsmiths	2	2	3a	3
Huddersfield	4	2		
Hull	3a	4	4	3
Keele	4	3	4	-
Kent	3b	3	5	5
Lancaster	5	4		
Leeds Met			3b	3
Leicester	4	3	3a	-
Lincs/Humberside			3b	1
Liverpool	3a	1		
Liverpool John Moores	2	-	3b	-
LSE			5*	5
London Guildhall			2	-
Luton	3b	-	2	-
Manchester			4	-
Manchester Metropolitan	2	-		
Middlesex	3b	2	4	-
Newcastle			3a	2
North London			2	2
Northumbria			3b	2
Open			4	3
Oxford			3a	-
Portsmouth			3b	2
Royal Holloway			3a	3
St Martins			1	-
Sheffield			4	4
Sheffield Hallam			3b	2
Southampton	3a	3		
South Bank			4	3
Staffordshire	2	-		
Sunderland			2	2
Sussex			3a	2
Thames Valley			3b	2
Warwick	5	3		
York	5	3	5	5
Dundee	3a	3		
Edinburgh	4	3	4	3
Glasgow			4	
Glasgow Caledonian			2	-
Stirling	5*	5		
Glamorgan			3b	-
Wales Bangor			4	3
NE Wales Institute	2	-		
Wales Newport			1	-
Wales Swansea	4	2		
Queen's Belfast	3a	2	3b	-
Ulster	3b	-	4	4

(Source: HEFCs)

106

References

Beresford, P. and Wallcroft, J. (1997) 'Psychiatric system survivors and emancipatory research: issues, overlaps and differences', in Barnes, C. and Mercer, G. (eds.) *Doing Disability Research*, Leeds: The Disability Press. 67-87.

Carew, R. (1979) 'The place of knowledge in social work activity', *British Journal of Social Work*, 9, 3, 349-64.

Cheetham, J. and Deakin, N. (1997) 'Research Note: Assessing the assessment: some reflections on the 1996 Higher Education Funding Council's Research Assessment Exercise', *British Journal of Social Work*, 27, 435-42.

Craig, G. (1997) *Quality First? The Assessment of Quality in Social Policy Research*, London: Social Policy Association.

Department of Health and Social Security (1985) *Social Work Decisions in Child Care*, London: HMSO.

Department of Health (1994) *A Wider Strategy for Research and Development relating to Personal Social Services*, London: HMSO.

Eraut, M. (1994) *Developing Professional Knowledge and Competence*, London: Falmer Press.

Evans, C. and Fisher, M. (1998a) 'Collaborative evaluation with service users', in Shaw, I. and Lishman, J. (eds.) *Evaluation and Social Work Practice*, London: Sage, forthcoming.

Evans, C. and Fisher, M. (1998b) 'User controlled research and empowerment', in Shera, W. and Wells, L. (eds.), *Empowerment Practice in Social Work: Developing Richer Conceptual Foundations*, Faculty of Social Work, University of Toronto, forthcoming.

Fisher, M. (1998) 'Research, knowledge and practice in community care', *Issues in Social Work Education*, 17, 2, 17-30.

Fisher, M., Marsh, P. and Phillips, D. (1986) *In and Out of Care*, London: Batsford.

Lewis, J. and Glennerster, H. (1996) *Implementing the New Community Care*, Buckingham: Open University Press.

Lyons, K. (1997) *Social Work and the Research Assessment Exercise 1996, Report to JUC/SWEC Research Sub-Committee*, JUC/SWEC.

Marsh, P. and Triseliotis, J. (1996) *Ready to Practise? Social Workers and Probation Officers: Their Training and First Year in Work*, Aldershot: Avebury.

Millham, S., Bullock, R., Hosie, K. and Haak, M. (1986) *Lost in Care: the Problem of Maintaining Links between Children in Care and Their Families*, Aldershot: Gower.

Pearson, G. (1975) *The Deviant Imagination: Psychiatry, Social Work and Social Change*, London: Macmillan.

Philp, M. (1979) 'Notes on the form of knowledge in social work', *Sociological Review*, 27, 1, 83-111.

Sainsbury, E. (1975) *Social Work with Families*, London: Routledge and Kegan Paul.

Sainsbury, E., Nixon, S. and Phillips, D. (1982) *Social Work In Focus*, London: Routledge and Kegan Paul.

Schön, D. (1995) 'Reflective inquiry in social work practice', in McCartt-Hess, P. and Mullen, E. (eds.) *Practitioner-Researcher Partnerships: Building Knowledge from, in and for Practice*, Washington D.C.: NASW Press. 31-55.

Sibeon, R. (1990) 'Social work knowledge, social actors and deprofessionalisation', in Abbot, P. and Wallace, C. (eds.) *The Sociology of the Caring Professions*, Basingstoke: Falmer Press. 90-111.

Social Work Research Association (1995) *Comment on 1996 RAE: Draft criteria for assessment and method of operation*.

Strauss, A. (1995) 'Notes on the nature and development of general theories', *Qualitative Inquiry*, 1, 1.

Chapter 8
Seeing the trees for the wood:
the politics of evaluating in practice

Ian Shaw

Sentimentality, superstition, and myth

When it comes to matters of research and evaluation, social workers are vulnerable to sentimentality, marked by a nurturing of myths and a tendency to superstitious practices.

We are guilty of sentimentality, says Howard Becker,

> 'when we refuse, for whatever reason, to investigate some matter that should properly be regarded as problematic. We are sentimental especially, when our reason is that we would prefer not to know what is going on, if to know would be to violate some sympathy whose existence we may not even be aware of' (Becker, 1970, 132-3).

The sentimentalities and superstitious practices that are of particular concern here are those most closely associated with this contributor's own commitments. The criticisms that make up the bulk of this chapter are drawn from a context in which this contributor is firmly committed to developing evaluation as a dimension of direct social work practice (Shaw, 1996, 1997). *Qualitative* evaluation offers a promising way forward to achieve evaluating-in-practice. Participatory and collaborative methods, the cultivation of a reflexive practice, egalitarian engagements between researchers and academics in higher education and social workers, and the potential of work-based assessment methods in post-qualifying social work programmes, are pointers to ways qualitative evaluating in practice can be developed.

This author is fully committed to, listening to, and learning from, the case made for *emancipatory*, praxis-oriented evaluation, to evaluating for and with service users, and to being strongly influenced by feminists' arguments that women, as outsiders on the inside, 'occupy a special status – they become different people, and their difference sensitises them to patterns that may be more difficult for established insiders to see' (Collins, 1986, p S29). This is a debt which must not be neglected.

There is a need to develop a richer and more rigorous *empirical base* for such evaluation including the need to give practitioners a voice in talking about ways in which they evaluate their day-to-day practice (Shaw and Shaw, 1997a, 1997b). It is important not to regard this as simply a preliminary ground-clearing exercise, filling in the gaps of research knowledge that have hitherto been neglected in the social work research and evaluation enterprise, but as a continuing normative obligation. It is important to listen carefully when leaders of the empirical practice movement challenge social workers and social scientists committed to humanist, qualitative, and participatory methodologies to begin detailing how they can be applied in practice.

And yet those who share these broad commitments are not immune from sentimentality, superstitious practices, and myth making. There are three particular 'myth stories' which cause concern and which will be touched on in this chapter.

- Quantitative methodology is politically manipulative, while qualitative methodology is not.

- Mainstream ('malestream') research and evaluation methods are politically manipulative while feminist methods are not.

- Expert, mainstream research and evaluation methods are politically manipulative, while emancipatory evaluation is not.

There are risks in embarking on such a course and this chapter is offered in a spirit of guarded reciprocal dialogue. Such exercises in guarded reciprocity should aspire to an outcome not too dissimilar from that described by Popper when he concluded that,

'Ironically enough, objectivity is closely bound up with the *social aspect of scientific method*, with the fact that science and scientific objectivity do not (and cannot) result from the attempts of an individual scientist to be 'objective', but from the *friendly-hostile co-operation of many scientists*. Scientific objectivity can be described as the inter-subjectivity of scientific method' (emphasis original).(Popper, 1966, Vol. II, p 217)

Quantitative v. qualitative

Anecdotal impressions suggest that rejection of quantitative methods among many student social workers and practitioners is rather akin to popular images of the debate regarding evolution versus creation as an explanation of the origins of life. It is known that there are still some folk who practise quantitative methodology, but they are regarded as 'off the wall' and quirky survivors of a bygone age. News of the nascent revival of positivist epistemology, and enthusiasm regarding the pay-offs from experimental research designs, has yet to spread. The late 1990s have witnessed an enthusiasm for evidence-based practice, coming on the back of the more influential moves towards evidence-based medicine. Evidence-based practice has been given regional and national infrastructures through the 'What Works' conferences in the Probation Service, the formation of the Centre for Evidence Based Social Services Research at Exeter University, and Research in Practice (an initiative of the Association of Directors of Social Services aimed at the improvement and dissemination of child care research).[2] None the less, the majority of social workers are incorrigible 'lovers of small numbers'[3], and will remain ready to embrace any of the several rationales for concluding that quantitative methodology is politically manipulative.

The choice is a serious one that extends far beyond a merely technical judgement about which research methodology produces the best results. In social work the model of research that dominated until the mid-1960s was a Fabian and democratic socialist policy research model, in which research was addressed – typically through survey methods – to the resolution of particular policy problems. The role of the researcher was seen as that of a social critic who would enlighten policy makers, agency managers, and practitioners (cf. Bulmer, 1982; Shaw, 1996, chapter 2).

Social work research was increasingly influenced by two developments from the mid-1960s. First, there was the growth of Marxism. While Marxist practice had a weak empirical agenda, influence out of proportion to its scale was exercised through exemplar research such as Paul Willis's *Learning to Labour* (Willis, 1977), and the dominant model of action research which emerged in the Home-Office-funded Community Development Projects (cf. Specht, 1976). Second, qualitative research, especially symbolic interactionism, began to emerge from the shadows of mainstream research. The precise reasons for this development have still to be documented in relation to social work, but the rapid expansion of university sociology degrees, and the perceived failure of randomised control group experiments first in America (e.g. Meyer, Borgatta and Jones, 1965) and subsequently in Britain (e.g. Goldberg, 1970) both played a part. Qualitative research was enriched by symbolic interactionist methodology books such as Denzin's *Research Act* (1970), which exercised a formative influence on several researchers who were later to become key figures in the social work research 'establishment'. It is only a slight oversimplification to observe also that the discipline of anthropology became transmuted in these years from a study of exotic societies into ethnography for urban society. The stronger emergence of qualitative sociologies in the field of education also exercised an indirect and seriously under-emphasised influence on social work developments (and do so now). It is probable also that Labour governments in the 1960s and early 1970s facilitated a growing role for evaluation research.

Following this period, qualitative research and evaluation developed into three different strands. First, *critical ethnographies* of social work represented a radicalisation of the earlier model of social research in which the researcher's role was that of social critic. Much of this work was done on the fringes of mainstream social work in fields such as youth work and community work. Harvey has reviewed some of this work (Harvey, 1990). From the late 1980s this strand has developed into broader liberatory and *activist qualitative models* of research, influenced from within social work by the shift in critical attention from social class to issues of race, gender, and disability. The influence of theorising about feminist standpoint, sketched in the next part of the chapter, has been one important driving force behind such developments.

The second strand is that of *interactionist ethnographies*. There have been few such ethnographies in social work, compared with medicine and education. Juvenile justice research was one strand in this work (e.g. Cicourel, 1968). (Ed. More recently another criminal justice study, on inner city probation work, drew heavily on interactionist and ethnographic understandings [Broad, 1991].) A central focus of ethnographic social work studies (e.g. Pithouse, 1988) has been on discipline development, although a critical perspective on practice was never absent (e.g. Rees, 1978). From the mid-1980s this strand was subject to the growing influence of relativism and scepticism about epistemology. Guba and Lincoln's *Fourth Generation Evaluation* (1989) has been a central text in this development, along with subsequent ones in feminist postmodernism (e.g. Hekman, 1990), thus bridging trends in both ethnography and evaluation.

Third, there has been the gradual emergence of *qualitative evaluation* in social work. Until very recently social workers have omitted different forms of evaluation, and qualitative forms have had no clear separate identity. Thus practitioner research in Britain and the scientific practitioner movement in the USA have been governed by a strongly utilitarian view of research and evaluation, in which matters of epistemology and methodology have been treated as important but essentially subordinate to pragmatic concerns about process and outcome of services (cf. Fuller and Petch, 1995; Cheetham, 1998). However, there have been several attempts at synthesising developments in qualitative social work evaluation (e.g. Sherman and Reid, 1994; Shaw, 1996; White, 1998), and the writing and research generated by these, together with the current interest in emancipatory evaluation, are likely to make this area volatile for the next few years.

The risk of superstition and sentimentality arises when social workers committed to a qualitative stance generalise in undifferentiated ways about the role of research and evaluation. In doing so they are liable to misrepresent its impact and benefits. For example, I am very uncomfortable with social work attacks on positivism and quantitative methodology. Take the following not untypical comments selected from a student text:

'Positivists not only see their work as uncontaminated: they see themselves as pure and safe in their objectivity, an élite who have managed to transcend the constraints of subjectivity.'

A problem of 'the positivist paradigm' is that

'the research endeavour is mystified; esoteric skills and techniques serve the interests of the powerful'.

'the essential values of positivism, objectivity, neutrality and determinism are . . . at variance with the value base, and the purposeful and humble activities of social work practice'.

Those whose research is framed by positivism are said to be guilty of

'spurious and dangerously simplistic solutions'.

(Everitt, Hardiker, Littlewood and Mullender, 1992, pp 6, 35, 55, 61; Mullender, Everitt, Hardiker and Littlewood, 1993-4, p 13)

Generalisations of this kind simply do not do justice to the problem. They caricature by omission the highly varied philosophical work that has been done in this field, betraying apparent unawareness of the far from straightforward arguments regarding objectivity, subjectivity, neutrality, and determinism that are part and parcel of the position they target. Being 'dangerously simplistic' follows from superstitious myth-making wherever it occurs. These writers echo that 'weary critique of positivism' in the early 1980s, which in Silverman's view more or less lacked coherence outside the pages of under-graduate examination books (Silverman, 1997, p 241). The omission of any discussion of critical realism, and failure to glimpse the radical discontinuities between positivism and most postpositivist positions, illustrates both the wearying character and lack of incoherence of which Silverman complains.

Take, for example, the use in this context of the word 'paradigm'. It is unhelpful in that it implies that all the characteristics of positivism come as a package, and also that there are no internal differences. 'It obscures both potential and actual diversity in orientation, and can lead us into making simplistic methodological decisions' (Hammersley, 1995, p 3). When 'quantitative' and 'qualitative' are characterised as paradigms they are usually set against one another as polar opposites, with the diversity within both equally hidden. For example, emancipatory evaluations and interactionist ethnographies both fall within qualitative methodology, yet they take very different positions on a wide range of paradigm-like issues such as relations to practitioners, theorising, the potential for policy applications, and political involvement.

An associated problem is that committed advocates of qualitative evaluation research are prone to assume a too close association between epistemology and methodology. The tacit assumption is that evaluators can and do choose methodologies consistent with their epistemology. There has been an extensive debate especially in American literature regarding paradigms, with the debate ranging from the pragmatism of Patton and Firestone to the paradigm commitment of Guba and Lincoln, and Smith (Firestone, 1990; Guba, 1990; Smith and Hershuis, 1986; Patton, 1990). While there is no easy solution (see Greene, 1994, for a helpful assessment), the implicit and unquestioned strong paradigm position in some British advocacy of qualitative methods smacks of sentimentality. Furthermore, it unhelpfully shifts the focus of attention too far away from methodological concerns towards broader interpretative issues.

Feminist v. malestream

It would provide 'aid and comfort to the barbarians' (Weiss, 1987) if the arguments of the previous paragraphs were hijacked, either to protect some advocates of quantitative methodologies from criticism on the grounds of their own sentimental and superstitious thinking and practices, or to reject the central thrust of feminist argument. The influence of feminism in many spheres of social work practice, research, and teaching has been almost breathtaking. For example 'feminism has literally revolutionised our sense of what today must count as "adequate" approximations to knowledge' (McLennan, 1995, p 397).

There are two main positions within feminist social work : feminist standpoint theory, and postmodern feminism.[4] *Feminist standpoint theory*

> 'disputes the traditional picture of science by proposing that the main-
> stream notion of scientific rationality is itself intrinsically masculinist,
> and thus not amenable to piecemeal correction by feminist scientists. On
> the contrary, feminists must openly abandon the quest for better
> "neutral" knowledge, replacing it with a clear emancipatory commit-
> ment to knowledge from the standpoint of women's experience and
> feminist theory' (McLennan, 1995, p 392).

It draws its rationale from the arguments of Hartsock, Harding, and others and starts from Marx's position that a correct vision of society is available only from one of the two major class positions in capitalist society.

Hartsock, in a classic paper, reworks Marxist arguments about the division of labour to apply to the sexual division of labour, in which girls define themselves *relationally*, while boys do not. She develops her position to claim that these different experiences are replicated in later life as epistemological and ontological differences. This male experience replicates itself in the institutions of class society.

Hartsock notes that, given the power of the controlling group to define the terms for the community as a whole, a feminist standpoint is *achieved* rather than obvious. 'The standpoint of the oppressed represents an achievement both of science (analysis) and of political struggle on the basis of which this analysis can be conducted' (Hartsock, 1983 p 288). It is a potentially hopeful position in that

> 'because it provides the basis for revealing the perversion of life and
> thought, the inhumanity of human relations, a standpoint can be the basis
> for moving beyond these relations. . . . (A) standpoint by definition
> carries a liberatory potential' (Hartsock, 1983, p 289).

Put simply, in response to the patriarchal assumption that women are less able to understand, standpoint theory argues that they are *more* able to do so. It does so through two linked assertions, the double vision of the oppressed and the partial vision of the powerful – 'privilege and its invisibility to those who hold it' (Swigonski, 1993, p 174).

Feminist standpoint theory when applied to social work evaluation espouses – if such a politically shaky verb may be used – a number of defining positions:

● Women's experience is seen as a more complete and less distorting kind of social experience.

● Objectivity is rejected for its inherent masculinist biases and distortions.

● Hierarchy within the research relationship is rejected as not simply bad method, but more importantly as both bad ethics and bad politics.

● An activist and empowerment conception of evaluation is implied, as undertaken for explicitly political purposes. 'The research process itself can become a process of "conscientisation" for both the researcher and the subjects of the research' (Cook and Fonow, 1990, p 75). In a much quoted comment Cook and Fonow say, 'The purpose of knowledge is to change or transform patriarchy. . . . Description without an eye for transformation is inherently conservative' (p 79).

The risk of superstition arises once unresolved aspects of feminist standpoint theory are treated by social workers as unproblematic and therefore are prone to being sentimentalised. There are three problems regarding feminist standpoint theory which have received growing attention in the literature, but which social work standpoint theorists such as Swigonski fail to 'problematise'.

First, there is an unresolved ambivalence within feminist standpoint theory, especially in regard to criticisms of objectivity (McLennan, 1995).

Second, as is by now well known, the argument for a privileged feminist perspective has been criticised from within feminist scholarship. For example, to Hawkesworth the idea 'appears to be highly implausible'. 'Given the diversity and fallibility of all human knowers, there is no good reason to believe that women are any less prone to error, deception or distortion than men' (Hawkesworth, 1989, p 544).

Third, standpoint theory has been criticised for 'essentialising' the concept of 'woman'. Third world, black, and Lesbian feminisms have together served to 'dissolve the conceptualisation of "woman" ' (Olesen, 1994, p 160). This creates problems for those who wish to argue that women's experience should have privileged status.

Standpoint theory is pulled one way by the realisation that, while affirming a radically different agenda for *what counts* as objective, it yet retains a search for universalising validation, and a different way by the emphasis on the diversity of women's experiences. Thus, while Gelsthorpe wishes to retain the terminology of standpoint theory, there is little remaining of its substance when she concludes,

> 'We cannot assume that black/white, young/old, and so on, experience life in the same way. . . . (We) choose standpoints and standpoints may change over time; they are transitional, not fixed points. . . . This leads me to argue that women do have uniquely valid insights from their vantage points as women, but women are never just women...The same goes for men, of course . . .' (Gelsthorpe, 1992, p 215).

This kind of argument reflects the important influence of the second main position within feminist social work, *feminist postmodernism*. There is an important feminist postmodern strand in British social work, in which the work of Susan Hekman has been especially influential (Hekman, 1990). While it is difficult to be conclusive, it is likely that there has been a move away from standpoint feminism in social work, and that the position of Hekman and others captures the main motif of feminist social work in Britain at the turn of the century, at least within higher education. Millen expresses it thus:

'Instead of privileging female or feminine standpoint, feminist postmodernism suggests that there is a variety of contradictory and conflicting standpoints, of social discourses, none of which should be privileged: there is no point in trying to construct a standpoint theory which will give us a better, fuller . . . knowledge because such knowledge does not exist' (Millen, 1997, 7.7).

While there are important variations within feminist postmodernism, stemming in part from ambiguity about what being postmodern entails, there are several recurring themes[5].

- a movement away from 'essentialising' concepts of women.

- A rejection of objectivism in favour of relativism.

- An engagement with pluralist and humanist research methodologies.

- A determination to politicise postmodernism and rescue it from any risk of political complacency.

- A strong claim that all knowledge is contextual and historically specific, and hence a hostility to cross-cultural explanations.

- A rejection of epistemology in exchange for discourse and rhetoric.

Our concern here is not primarily with the arguments of feminist postmodernism as such, any more than with the arguments of feminist standpoint theory, but with the constant risk that the advocacy of a methodology that expresses core beliefs will be prone to a failure to 'problematise', and thus a risk of superstitious sentimentality. We referred earlier to the hazards of using 'paradigm' language to attack perceived enemies. In addition, there is the danger that broad-brush arguments will be used to bury rather than praise contrary positions, in the way we illustrated earlier in this chapter. For example, there is a tendency in too much feminist work to caricature the position of modernist researchers, through allegations that they aspire to absolute truth through research, and that they claim it is possible to hold 'God's eye view' (cf. Hekman, 1990, pp 152-3; Nicholson, 1990, pp 2,3).

Relativist positions have also been troubled by practitioner struggles. Jennifer Greene is one of a number of people working from an educational context who have sharpened our understanding of qualitative approaches to evaluation.

'Many qualitative practitioners struggle with the dissonance invoked by the assumed mind-dependence of all social knowledge claims in the face of the contextual (as well as personal, ego-related) demands to "*get it right*", to "*find out what's really going on in this setting*" (Greene, 1996, p 280. Emphasis in original).

A distinction needs drawing between 'strong' and 'partial' postmodernist positions. A strong position probably would adopt unequivocally all six of the above themes. In practice, it is likely that a range of more-partial positions is being advocated, without always acknowledging the unresolved tensions that exist between them. If this is a fair reading, then it would help explain why postmodern statements sometimes seem to hedge their bets. For example, Millen asks, 'How can we propose a political philosophy without some sort of epistemic unity?' (1997, 7.8). She clings to the aspiration that:

'A dual role, where we use postmodern insights to continually critique the role of feminist research and the gendered aspects of mainstream research, but utilise modernist ideas to advance feminism's political agenda, may be possible' (1997, 7.10).

She adds an immediate postscript that 'consensus is not, after all, a primary aim of feminism'. Millen makes a valuable point. We should beware of the chronic scepticism that marks epistemological purists. It is quite appropriate to be caught between different paradigms if this reflects the constituency of which we are a part. Indeed, it is likely to be a creative, if anxious, experience. To ask for a cut-and-dried position risks provoking accusations of the very masculinist thinking referred to earlier! But accepting unresolved diversity is still a problematic position for feminist evaluators, researchers, and social workers. McLennan asks, in this context, if a hesitation in abandoning epistemic grounding may be due to 'the premonition that feminism as a distinctive theory and practice might dissolve with its absorption into postmodernism' (1995, p 393).

Emancipatory v. Mainstream
There is a problem common to both feminist and emancipatory research. It was noted that hierarchy within the research relationship is rejected by feminist analysis and practice as not simply bad method but more importantly as both bad ethics and bad politics. However, there has been widening acknowledgement that activist research is not immune from the paradox and irony that 'our efforts to liberate perpetuate the relations of dominance' (Humphries, 1997, 3.5). For example, in a reflexive account of her own research in which she asks whether there can be a feminist ethnography, Stacey wonders 'whether the appearance of greater respect for and equality with research subjects in the

ethnographic approach masks a deeper, more dangerous form of exploitation'. She concludes that 'conflicts of interest between the ethnographer as authentic, related person (i.e. participant), and as exploiting researcher (i.e. observer)' are 'an inescapable feature of the ethnographic method' (Stacey, 1988, p 22). She exemplifies the plea that in making women's lives problematic feminists 'should not turn away from rendering their own practices problematic' (Olesen, 1994, p 169) in her suggestion that feminists tend to suffer the 'delusion of alliance' (1988, p 23). Martin (1994 and 1996) and Whitmore (1994) have portrayed this problem in participative research in areas of relevance to social work.

There is a welcome recent willingness, in Lather's apposite phrase, to 'protect our work from our own passions' (Lather, 1986a, p 77). Humphries goes as far as to say that both traditional research and emancipatory research need to be interrogated 'and *both* may be found wanting' (1997, 4.6). She asks 'surely it is possible to recognise the particularities of struggle without abandoning the metanarratives of emancipation and justice' (4.8). In so doing there is a need to acknowledge 'the permanent partiality of the point of view of those of us seeking to construct emancipatory research', and that 'an emancipatory intent is no guarantee of an emancipatory outcome' (4.8, 4.10).

> 'In sum, the development of emancipatory social theory requires an empirical stance which is open-minded, dialogically reciprocal, grounded in respect for human capacity, and yet profoundly sceptical of appearances and "common sense" ' (Lather, 1986b, p 269).

Lather's transparent commitment displays both welcome aspiration and yet the recurrent risk once more of sentimentality on the part of liberatory researchers. Lather's vigorous warnings against the theoretical imperialism within neo-Marxism – the 'circle where theory is reinforced by experience conditioned by theory' (Lather, 1986b, p 261) – are salutary. 'Theory is too often used to protect us from the awesome complexity of the world' and

> 'neo-Marxist praxis-oriented work too often falls prey to . . . the irony of domination and repression inherent in most of our efforts to free one another. . . . In the name of emancipation, researchers impose meanings on situations rather than constructing meaning through negotiation with research participants' (1986b, pp 267, 265).

'Open-minded' research and evaluation present an unresolved tension within a tradition where too often 'one is left with the impression that the research conducted provides empirical specificities for more general, *a priori* theories' (Lather, 1986a, p 76). Her desire for 'dialogically reciprocal' research is open to similar ambiguities. She openly admits to 'a lack of self-reflexivity in the empirical work that exists within critical inquiry. . . . Too often, critical self-awareness comes to mean a negative attitude to competing approaches instead of its own self-critical perspective' (1986a, p 65).

Conclusion

The concern throughout this chapter has been with the risks that attach to a commitment to qualitative and emancipatory evaluation. The tensions will not go away. Lather is arguing for a reworked neo-Marxist position yet she catches pointedly the tensions that face all social work evaluation if it is to escape the risks of sentimentality, superstition, and myth making that are its constant temptation. Those engaging in research cannot retreat to the older traditions of research and evaluation where the applications of uses of research were only the vaguest responsibility of researchers themselves. The demands of social justice and citizenship challenge all political sentimentalities. There is no 'Blue Peter' template for applying these demands. Yet unless there is

'an engaged, accountable . . . scientific citizenship, I fear that qualitative evaluation will be relegated to the sidelines of important debates about public issues. . . . No longer can we shroud our citizen-selves behind our scientific subjectivities. We must become scientific citizens' (Greene, 1996, pp 286-7).

Notes

(1) Positivism, in social work at least, is no longer 'a swearword by which no-one is swearing' (Williams, 1976: 239). It is still a swearword, as we go on to illustrate, but there is a small but vocal number of advocates willing to swear by the merits of positivism for social work (see, for example, Thyer, 1989, 1993; Rotheray, 1993).

(2) 'Evidence-based practice' has, in fact, both a narrow and a wider usage. The two usages have a large area of overlap. The broader meaning is marked by emphases on the obligation of social workers to ground their practice judgements in explicit evidence, a more explicit drawing on research findings, and a determination to disseminate research findings and make them accessible. It also includes an emphasis on outcome research rather than research about process, and a generally positive belief in the potential to apply research to practice and policy in an incremental fashion. The narrower sense of the term includes all of these features, but also typically includes a negativity towards qualitative research and evaluation, and an advocacy of particular methods of practice intervention (usually cognitive or behaviourally based). I have criticised the narrower concept in Shaw, 1996 (Chapters Five and Nine) and Shaw and Shaw, 1997b.

(3) The phrase is W H Auden's from his poem 'Numbers and Faces' 'Lovers of small numbers go benignly potty. . . . Lovers of big numbers go horridly mad. . .'

(4) Until recently it was customary also to include feminist empiricism as a third position. Feminist empiricism seeks to criticise male ways of knowing from within a traditional position of science as a potentially objective knowledge form, and thus provide an empirical corrective to male bias. However, there has been forceful and generally persuasive criticism to the effect that, at least in epistemological terms, feminist empiricism as a category 'does not really exist at all: either you have women empiricists or feminist standpoint epistemologists' (McLennan, 1995, p 396).

(5) I am indebted to McLennan's influential essay at this point (McLennan, 1995). In addition, Hekman (1990), Flax (1990), Nicholson (1990), and Rorty (1991) represent important work.

References

Becker, H (1970) *Sociological Work* New York, Aldine.

Broad, B (1991) *Punishment under Pressure: the Probation Service in the Inner City: London*, Jessica Kingsley.

Bulmer, M (1982) *The Uses of Social Research* London, Allen and Unwin.

Cheetham, J (1998) 'The evaluation of social work: priorities, problems and possibilities', in Cheetham, J. and Kazi, M (eds.), *The Working of Social Work*, London, Jessica Kingsley.

Cicourel, A (1968) *The Social Organisation of Juvenile Justice* New York, John Wiley.

Collins, P (1986) 'Learning from the Outside Within: the Sociological Significance of Black Feminist Thought' *Social Problems*, 33 (6) pp S14-S32.

Cook, J and Fonow, M (1990) 'Knowledge and Women's Interests: Issues of Epistemology and Methodology in Feminist Sociological Research' in Neilsen, J (ed.) *Feminist Research Methods* New York, Westview Press, pp 69-93.

Denzin, N (1970) *The Research Act in Sociology* Chicago, Aldine.

Everitt, A, Hardiker, P, Littlewood, J and Mullender, A (1992) *Applied Research for Better Practice* London, Macmillan.

Firestone, W (1990) 'Accommodation: Towards a paradigm-praxis dialectic' in Guba, E (ed.) *The Paradigm Dialog* Newbury Park, Sage, pp 105-124.

Flax, J (1990) *Thinking Fragments* Berkeley, University of California Press.

Fuller, R and Petch, A (1995) *Practitioner Research* Buckingham, Open University Press.

Gelsthorpe, L (1992) 'Response to Martin Hammersley's paper on feminist methodology' *Sociology*, 26, (2) pp 213-18.

Goldberg, E (1970) *Helping the Aged* London, Allen and Unwin.

Greene, J (1994) 'Qualitative Program Evaluation: Practice and Promise', in Denzin, N and Lincoln Y (eds.), *Handbook of Qualitative Methodology*, Thousand Oaks, Sage, pp 530-544.

Greene, J (1996) 'Qualitative Evaluation and Scientific Citizenship' *Evaluation*, 2 (3), pp 277-289.

Guba, E (1990) (ed.) *The Paradigm Dialog* Newbury Park, Sage.

Guba, E and Lincoln, Y (1989) *Fourth Generation Evaluation* Newbury Park, Sage.

Hammersley, M (1995) *The Politics of Social Research* London, Sage.

Hammersley, M (1997) 'A reply to Humphries' *Sociological Research Online* 2 (4), <http://www.socresonline.org.uk/socresonline/2/4/6.html>.

Harding, S (1987) (ed.) Feminism and Methodology, Buckingham, Open University Press.

Hartsock, N (1983) 'The feminist standpoint: developing the ground for a specifically feminist historical materialism, in Harding, S and Hintikka, M (eds.) *Discovering Reality* Dordrecht, Reidl Publishing.

Harvey, L. (1990), *Critical Social Research*, London, Unwin Hyman.

Hawkesworth, M (1989) 'Knowers, knowing, known: Feminist theory and claims of truth' *Signs: Journal of Women in Culture and Society* 14 (3) pp 533-555.

Hekman, S (1990), *Gender and Knowledge: Elements of a Postmodern Feminism*, Cambridge, Policy Press.

Humphries, B (1997) 'From critical thought to emancipatory action: Contradictory research goals?' *Sociological Research Online* 2 (1) <http:www.socresonline.org.uk/socresonline/2/1/3.html>.

Kirk, S (1990) 'Research utilisation: the substructure of belief', in Videka-Sherman, L and Reid, W (eds.) *Advances in Clinical Social Work Research* Washington, NASW, pp 233-250.

Lather, P (1986a) 'Issues of validity in openly ideological research' *Interchange* 17 (4) pp 63-84.

Lather, P (1986b) 'Research as praxis' *Harvard Educational Review* 56 (3) pp 257-77.

Martin, M (1994) 'Developing a feminist participative research framework' in Humphries, B and Truman, C (eds.) *Rethinking Social Research: Anti-Discriminatory Approaches in Research Methodology* Aldershot, Hants, Avebury.

Martin, M (1996) 'Issues of power in the participatory research process' in de Koning, K and Martin, M (eds.) *Participatory research in health* London, Zed Books, pp 82-93.

McLennan, G (1995) 'Feminism, epistemology and postmodernism: Reflections on current ambivalence' *Sociology*, 29, (2), pp 391-409.

Meyer, C (1992) 'Social work assessment: Is there an empirical base?' *Research on Social Work Practic*e, 2 (3), pp 297-305.

Meyer, C (1996) 'My son the scientist' *Social Work Research* 20 (2), pp 101-104.

Meyer, H, Borgatta, E and Jones W (1965) *Girls at Vocational High* New York, Russell Sage Foundation.

Miller, J (1992) 'Exploring power and authority issues in a collaborative research project' *Theory and Practice* 21 (2), pp 165-72.

Miller, J and Martens, M (1990) 'Hierarchy and imposition in collaborative inquiry: Teacher-researchers' reflections on recurrent dilemmas' *Educational Foundations*, 4 (4), pp 41-59.

Millen, D (1997) 'Some methodological and epistemological issues raised by doing feminist research on non-feminist women' *Sociological Research Online* 2 (3) <http:www.socresonline.org.uk/socresonline/2/3/3.html>.

Mullender, A, Everitt, A, Hardiker, P and Littlewood, J (1993-4) 'Value issues in research' *Social Action* 1 (4) pp 11-18.

Nicholson, L (1990) (ed.) *Feminism/Postmodernism* London, Routledge.

Olesen, V (1994) 'Feminisms and models of qualitative research' in Denzin, N and Lincoln, Y (eds.) *Handbook of Qualitative Methodology* Thousand Oaks, Sage, pp 158-74.

Patton, M (1990) *Qualitative Evaluation and Research Methods* Newbury Park, Sage.

Pithouse, A (1988) *Social Work: the Social Organisation of an Invisible Trade* Aldershot, Hants, Avebury.

Popper, K (1966) *The Open Society and Its Enemies*, Volume II, London, Routledge.

Rees, S (1978) *Social Work Face to Face* London, Edward Arnold.

Reid, W (forthcoming) 'Empirical practice' in Shaw, I and Lishman, J (eds.) *Evaluation and Social Work Practice*, London, Sage.

Rorty, R (1991) 'Feminism and postmodernism' *Radical Philosophy* 59, pp 3-14.

Rotheray. M (1993) 'The positivistic research approach' in Grinnell, R (ed.) *Social Work Research and Evaluation*, New York, F E Peacock.

Shadish, W, Cook, T and Leviton, L (1990) *Foundations of Program Evaluation: Theories of Practice* Newbury Park, Sage.

Shaw, I (1996) *Evaluating in Practice* Aldershot, Hants, Ashgate.

Shaw, I (1997) *Be Your Own Evaluator: A Guide to Reflective and Enabling Evaluating in Practice* Wrexham, Wales, Prospects Publishing.

Shaw, I (1998) 'Practising evaluating' in Cheetham, J and Kazi, M (eds.) *The Working of Social Work* London, Jessica Kingsley, pp 201-23.

Shaw, I and Shaw, A (1997a) 'Game plans, buzzes and sheer luck: doing well in social work' *Social Work Research* 21 (2), pp 69-79.

Shaw, I and Shaw A (1997b) 'Keeping social work honest: Evaluation as profession and practice' *British Journal of Social Work* 27 (6), 847-69.

Sherman, E and Reid, W (1994) *Qualitative Research in Social Work* New York, Columbia University Press.

Silverman, D (1997) 'Towards an aesthetics of research' in Silverman, D (ed.) *Qualitative Research*, London, Sage, pp 234-53.

Smith, J (1992) 'Interpretive inquiry: a practical and moral activity' *Theory into Practice* 31, (2) pp 100-6.

Smith, J and Hershuis, L (1986) 'Closing down the conversation: the end of the quantitative-qualitative debate among educational inquirers' *Educational Researcher* 15 (1), pp 4-12.

Specht, H (1976) *Community Development Projects* London, National Institute for Social Work Training.

Stacey, J (1988) 'Can there be a feminist ethnography?' *Women's Studies International Forum*, 11 (1), pp 21-27.

Swigonski, M (1993) 'Feminist standpoint theory and questions of social work research' *Affilia*, 8 (2) pp 171-83.

Thyer, B (1989) 'First principles of practice research' *British Journal of Social Work* 19 (4) pp 309-23.

Thyer, B (1993) 'Social Work Theory and Practice Research: the Approach of Logical Positivism' *Social Work and Social Sciences Review*, 4 (1), pp 5-26.

Weiss, C. (1987) 'Where politics and evaluation meet', in Palumbo, D J (ed.) *The Politics of Program Evaluation*, Newbury Park, Sage, pp 12-46.

White, S (1998) 'Analysing the content of social work: Applying the lessons of qualitative research' in Cheetham, J and Kazi, M (eds.) *The Working of Social Work* London, Jessica Kingsley, pp 153-69.

Whitmore, E (1994) 'To tell the truth: Working with oppressed groups in participatory approaches to inquiry' in Reason, P (ed.) *Participation in Human Inquiry*, London, Sage, pp 82-98

Williams, R (1976) *Keywords: a Vocabulary of Culture and Society* London, Fontana.

Willis, P (1977) *Learning to Labour: How Working Class Kids Get Working Class Jobs* Aldershot, Hants, Gower.

Chapter 9
A social action approach to research

Mark Harrison

In this chapter I will argue that positivist research has failed those who are the focus of its enquiries, whether community groups or service users, and that this is done by employing methods which impose the researchers' agenda, thereby ignoring the users' agenda. It follows, therefore, that if the research methodology used is inappropriate and flawed then the findings and the services that develop as a result will be the same. It will also be argued that the social policies and programmes emerging from traditional forms of research reflect the interests of the powerful rather than the communities and groups they will impact upon. The social action research approach is presented as a counter to the assumptions which guide positivist research, by it offering a progressive, user-led, responsive yet rigorous model for conducting research. Two examples of research using the approach are referred to illustrating the relationship between theory, values, practice, and research. The challenge for commissioners of research, policy makers, and politicians who are concerned with social equity is to adopt progressive models rather than the traditional conservative approaches preferred by academics and research institutions.

The origin and development of the social action model

The development of empowerment and social action models is relatively recent coinciding with powerful critiques of traditional research that have been elaborated by the women's movement (Oakley 1981), the black community (Gilroy 1992, Bourne and Sivananden 1991), and the disability rights movement (Oliver 1992), as well as by community development workers (Holman 1987, Beresford and Croft 1990,1993).

Oakley offers a critique of traditional social research, from a feminist perspective:

> Interviewers define the role of interviewees as subordinates: extracting information is more to be valued than yielding it: the convention of inter-viewer-interviewee hierarchy is a rationalisation of inequality; what is good for interviewers is not necessarily good for interviewees (Oakley 1981, p.40).

In relation to the black community Bourne offers three ways of moving away from traditional research which would enable it to make a contribution to combating racism

(i) a description of experience in the face of 'academics who abstract and distort black experience (however unwittingly)'; (ii) a redefinition of problem; and (iii) a challenge to the ideology and methodology of dominant research paradigms.

Oliver, who has written extensively about the need to establish a new research paradigm, says:

> This new paradigm must throw off the shackles of methodological individualism with its inadequate and abstracted view of the individual for emancipatory research can only be really accomplished. [*sic*], p 113

Holman in 1987 suggested some benchmarks, which have been subsequently reworked (Taylor 1997). They are:

- Who owns the research?
- Who defines the issues?
- Who decides how the topic should be researched?
- Who interprets the findings?
- What role do respondents play in data collection?
- For what purposes will the research be used?

It was then, in the late 1970s and early 1980s, that the relationship between the research and the researched began to be scrutinised. This led to the development of social action concepts and methodologies. This initiative emerged out of frustrations on the part of community members, service users, and some professionals at the failure of research and the resulting social policies to create significant social change. It has largely been led, not by the research community, but by frustrated and disillusioned community and service user groups. The starting point for social action is to offer a way forward for research that is rooted in practice and in a set of principles that empower rather than exploit community members and service users. Social action has developed this practice over the last 20 years. It came about through youth social workers and educators joining forces because they were dissatisfied with youth social work in general and youth justice policies in particular.

Out of this dialogue an approach emerged which rejected the value base and methods being employed by the mainstream professions and institutions responsible for social and urban policy. It became clear that the problems did not just lie in the policy and practices of institutions, whether in the voluntary or statutory sector. They were also rooted in the current education and training of professionals and the research models and methods that informed and shaped policy and practice.

Social action in context

The prevailing social policy ethos that guided government programmes in the 1970s/80s, based on 'underclass' theories, dominates many of today's influential academics and politicians. According to Murray the main threat to society comes from 'the underclass'. Three indicators are used to assess the extent of the problem: crime, illegitimacy, and economic inactivity among working-age men (Murray 1996). The consequent social policy proposals focused, for example, on policies such as penalising women for getting pregnant outside marriage. The welfare of society and indeed the survival of free institutions and civil society are presented as being 'at stake' . . . (Murray:1996,127). The acceptance of these underclass theories in the UK came nearly a decade ago (Field 1989). For the post-1987 New Labour government 'social exclusion' has once again been re-interpreted to focus more on symptoms rather than its causes: poverty, for example.

The current administration is proposing the greatest reform of the tax and benefits system since it was established and its vision is to create a 'third way' between unbridled individualism and *laissez-faire* on the one hand, and, on the other, old-style government intervention, the corporatism of the 1960s.

According to Williams (1998):

> The flagstones of the third way have been laid. Each has its American counterpart. They are welfare-to-work, the reform of the social security system, earned income tax credits, and the creation of a highly flexible and competitive workforce.

Underclass theories are now shaping and underpinning government policy (Davies 1997, pp.304), as seen most overtly in the changes to social security legislation in 1997. Their influence can also be seen in social programmes in the non-governmental sector. The investment of £1million by the Joseph Rowntree Foundation in the *Communities that Care* initiative demonstrates how established underclass theories have become. *Communities that Care* has been imported from America and is a child care programme that can be seen as a combination of highly professionalised (behaviourist) social work interventions and community development rhetoric. Similar influences can be seen in the criminal justice field where the government's 'zero tolerance' policies can be regarded as a continuation of the penal policies of the Conservative governments. It is argued here that these, and similar, underclass policies are the result of detailed theoretical work and empirical research using positivist research methodologies supporting Murray's hypothesis both that an underclass exists and that it is the cause of all societies' ills:

> 'Rather like the ideas of Hayek and others in the 1970's, this theory comes originally from the United States, from the fringes of intellectual thought, where it was popularised by an academic named Charles Murray. The theory is self-serving, in that is allows the affluent to justify more cuts to the welfare state which in turn will pay for more cuts in their own taxes. . . . And yet, despite its obvious flaws, the theory has been adopted by liberal journalists and Labour Politicians, by academics and commentators and think-tanks, and now flows over the centre ground just as the ideas of Hayek did nearly twenty years earlier' (Davies 1997).

The social action approach aims to provide a different perspective on the origin and definition of social conditions and circumstances and, therefore, the resolution of same.

Social action and grounded theory

Social action emerged in the late 1970s (Fleming *et al.*, 1983). The theoretical and practical inspirations underpinning social action come from the work of Paulo Freire and Saul Alinsky. In practical terms, lessons were learnt from community work, the experience of the Community Development Projects (CDPs) in the 1970s, and social education. Social action has also been influenced by the work and struggles of black writers and activists, notably George Jackson and Steve Biko. It was also inspired by the movement in youth culture and music, particularly Reggae, Punk, and Two Tone and drew strength and encouragement from the women's movement's challenge to the (male) authority and professionalism exerted over their lives. More recently the emergence of the disability rights movement, the Disability Action Network, and the writings of Mike Oliver and others have reaffirmed and deepened our commitment to challenging current orthodoxies in social and urban policy, practice and research. From this critique, analysis, and theoretical base was developed a framework for revolutionising practice.

Social action is a model of social care and intervention which turns the professional's role on its head (see Mullender and Ward 1991). Instead of being the provider and giver of all knowledge, wisdom, skills and services – which arguably, we cannot deliver anyway – the 'professionals' become facilitators, or social educators, where people are encouraged to:

1. set the agenda

2. analyse critically their situation

3. devise ways of tackling issues, problems, and concerns

4. take action for themselves

5. reflect on their experiences, consolidate their learning, and begin the process again on a higher level.

Community members and service users control the (subject) content, analysis, action, and reflection. The professional provides the framework or process. This approach, which has been developed and refined, is based on a set of values and principles.

Social action principles

● All people have skills and understanding which they can draw on to tackle the problems they face. Professionals should not attach negative labels to service users.

● All people should have rights, including the right to be heard, the right to define issues facing them, and the right to take action on their own behalf.

● People acting collectively can be powerful. People who lack power and influence can gain it through working together in groups. Practice should reflect this understanding.

● Individuals in difficulty are often confronted by complex issues rooted in social policy, the environment and the economy. Responses to them should reflect this understanding.

● Methods of working must reflect non-élitist principles. Workers do not 'lead' the group but facilitate members in making decisions for themselves and controlling whatever outcome ensues. Though special skills and knowledge are employed, these do not accord privilege and are not solely the province of the workers.

● Work must challenge inequality and discrimination in relation to race, gender, sexual orientation, age, class, disability, or any other form of social differentiation.

The Centre for Social Action, sited within the Department of Social and Community Studies at De Montfort University seeks to apply these principles in its work.

More generally, a number of groups were set up using the social action model: young people at risk and in trouble (young offenders), school 'refusers', unemployed young people, young people in care, punks, rock and reggae musicians, young Asian women, minority ethnic groups, young women with children. These young people have engaged in a wide variety of activities: for example, setting up and running their own youth club; challenging and changing the policing of their estate; planning and running their own businesses; influencing the plans for housing regeneration; challenging agency racism and sexism; setting up, running, and managing a peer education project around drug and health issues. This work has often happened with young people who are alienated and marginalised. They are often the ones who are labelled and written off.

Having established the parameters for practice and having begun to test it out, it became clear that this approach had wider applications for training and research. The existing training agencies were still instucting people in the old methods, values, and practices, so in looking for appropriate training it became clear to us that we would have to set this up for ourselves. More of the same would not do. The training process and methods we developed mirrored the social action process we carried out in the work.

The first part of this process is based on Freire's philosophy of praxis – critical reflection and human action (Freire 1972). It incorporates the notion that praxis is dialogue which consists of both action and reflection, or active reflection and reflective action, in an equal or balanced relationship. This dialogue breaks down the traditional relationship between teacher:student and the 'banking' concept of education and replaces it with a partnership where roles interchange and the teacher:student and student:teacher are co-investigators each reforming his or her thinking through reflecting one with the other. Knowledge is created or re-created through critical reasons.

The next component is *problematisation*, which is a process of drawing attention to situations that require action or change. The possibility of change is indicated by posing changes. Problem posing is a process of questioning deeper structures; of challenging commonly accepted ideas by posing more and more questions to dig beneath conventional or common-sense explanations of reality; of raising and analysing contradictions (Kidd and Kumar 1994).

The third and final component is *conscientisation*. This Freire describes as a permanent critical approach to reality in order to discover it and discover the myths that deceive us and help to maintain the oppressing dehumanising structures. It leaves nobody inactive (Freire 1972). Conscientisation goes beyond consciousness-raising or an awareness of reality and involves a critical development strategy from experience.

Social action has developed a five stage process based on Freire's coding system – naming, reflecting, and action. This *five stage process* is:

1.   What? – What are the issues, concerns, problems?
2.   Why? – Why do they exist?
3.   How? – How can this be changed?
4.   Action? – What action can be taken by the group?
5.   Reflection? – review process and action by repeating the five stages.

The social action model is elaborated more fully in Mullender and Ward (1991) and was adapted for training different groups.

Social action research in practice

Social action research begins from the premise that people, whether community members or service users, are not merely the object of research but become the subject of research. Treating people as subjects means they have the right to speak out and the right to be *heard*. This is part of the empowering and enabling social action principle. Yet this, by itself, is not innovatory so the social action research method involves subjects at all stages. This dialogue style of research provides a better understanding of different perceptions of service users and allows them to shape parameters of the research. Fleming and Ward (1995) explain this process in more detail:

> The social action research process starts with an open ended enquiry rather than with an attempt to verify existing ideas. Social action research does not start with preconceived ideas and concepts, rather we work with service users, managers and practitioners to identify the focus of the research and the outcomes it is seeking. These groups are involved in the refinement of the objectives for research or evaluation, in the formation of methods and in the interpretation of the data collected. We look to establish a collaborative method with all people affected by and involved in the research process.

This research process creates new agendas for change. It reverses the traditional way of carrying out research. Traditional research methods use quantitative research methods at the enquiry stage and qualitative methods to enrich the data collected. Social action research uses qualitative methods to establish with the service users, community or young people being studied, the parameters, areas, and content for research and the questions to be asked. Qualitative methods such as individual interviews and focus groups using guided interview schedules are then devised from the initial consultation process. Sometimes community members or young people are employed as researchers to facilitate this process, particularly when working with minority ethnic communities, supported by a social action research supervisor. (Dyson 1995, Dyson and Harrison 1997). They are trained, supported, and equipped to carry out the process by the research supervisor, often using a workshop format.

The results of this enquiry are then analysed, again using qualitative methods. These are fed back to the research subjects usually again in the form of a workshop to check findings and to ensure that the research process hasn't missed out anything essential.

By involving research subjects at every stage, including devising recommendations, there is a much higher validity and ownership of the findings. It also means the research process is an empowering one and creates agendas for change, which have meaning to both sponsors and subjects of the research. In this way the social action research process addresses the criticisms of traditional and conventional practices outlined at the beginning of this paper. It also offers practitioners and researchers a progressive and innovatory way forward.

I have previously argued (Harrison 1993), that socially excluded groups, by definition, do not have access to, and have rejected, the society that has failed them. To gain access and to work with these groups effectively they must be allowed and enabled to set their own agenda and take action for themselves. This theme has been developed in the first example, examining the experiences of two research projects that have worked alongside and in partnership with black and minority ethnic communities. The distinguishing feature of this work is that community members were the active researchers and the research institutions operated in a supporting role. The other example is a community consultation on child care carried out for Derby City Council and Barnardo's on the Sinfin estate.

Examples of social action research
(1) African Caribbean and Asian community, Leicester, and the Somali refugee community, East London
This research involved two parallel surveys of community awareness of sickle cell anaemia and beta-thalassaemia in Leicester (Dyson and Goyder, 1994a and 1994b). These two inherited blood disorders, (the haemoglobinopathies) particularly affect peoples of African-Caribbean and South Asian descent respectively, although both conditions are found to some extent in many other ethnic groups. The research interviews were conducted by members of the local self-help groups (the Organization for Sickle Cell Anaemia Research and the Thalassaemia Society) and generated several potential learning points for future research involving community members in the research process.

The approach was taken up and developed further in the second set of projects which related to work alongside the refugee Somali community in Tower

Hamlets in East London. This community is thought to number around 30,000 people, principally displaced by the civil wars in Somalia. Building on contacts made in the course of a research project identifying housing needs of refugees (Harrison, 1993), the Centre for Social Action was commissioned by the Tower Hamlets Race Equality Council (THREC) to look at the take-up of welfare services by the Somali community in the Bethnal Green City Challenge Area (Harrison *et al.*, 1995). This THREC project tried to take up learning points from the haemoglobinopathy surveys in employing members of the Somali community as researchers. The collection of data was preceded by a workshop based around 10 issues that had arisen in the Leicester surveys (Dyson 1995).

Issues for researchers arising from this project

General Points

1.   There are clearly important and defining reasons, why working in these ways should be considered appropriate, politically as well as professionally. Firstly, whether of African-Caribbean, South Asian or Somali descent, the interviewers have a common experience of racism. Involving community members as researchers recognises both that people have skills and understanding which they can bring to bear on their own circumstances, and permits at least the possibility that white workers may share their skills and not keep what Bourdieu characterises as cultural capital to themselves (Bourdieu and Passeron 1997).

2.   The research approach tries to avoid the problem of setting up black projects to fail. By not turning the research project over to black community members wholesale, leaving people unsupported in circumstances made challenging by economy, policy, environment, and racism the research institution does not abandon the community but negotiates a new relationship based on partnership.

3.   In connection with the processes of research, there are the issues of what may be termed research scepticism and research fatigue in the black communities. The former refers to the feeling that researchers take information from communities but those communities do not see the benefits of changes. The latter alludes to the degree of monitoring that can take place where marginal groups become the continued targets of researchers. Only by black and white workers successfully working together, it may be argued, can a situation be avoided whereby research participants are not themselves estranged from the research process (Oliver 1992). Only by conducting research that effects change and provides community feedback can the conditions for changing the social relations of research production (Oliver 1992) begin to be established.

135

Learning Points

The dialogue established between the two research supervisors led to a number of learning points and conclusions.

1. Reliability of data collected

   In both cases the quality and accuracy of data collected were enhanced by using community members as researchers. In the Somali case it was only Somali community members who could have gained access and collected data from the sections of their community who are the hardest to reach, i.e. elderly, warriors, single women.

2. Validity of data collected

   The critical reflections of the community interviewers on the validity of the findings they generate in support sessions should be an integral part of the data presentation. At the same time it is incumbent on the research supervisors to ensure that, for example, these validity checks are not mis interpreted by commissioning bodies as evidence of poor quality data, but to draw attention to the equivalent missing (or even suppressed?) checks in other data that a commissioning body may be relying upon. For example the census does not include a category for refugees but census data is used for planning services.

3. Paid work or voluntary effort

   The pros and cons of monetary payments for community research should be discussed with the community members at an early stage of planning. Where those members themselves feel that the team should be paid, and that payment is not compromising an important voluntary service ethos, then we feel that the following points should be addressed. The rates of pay should be on professional scales, but at a point of such scales reflecting both the level of research experience of the community members and the real level of hours the work involved, and with proper allowance made to adequately fund research training support and supervision.

4. Safety issues

   Particular attention needs to be paid to health and personal safety issues at the planning stage and to ensuring that community members are given at least the protection of identification and official documentation to carry with them in their work. Because much of the interviewing took place outside office hours – evenings and weekends – and in areas with a history of racial attacks, discussions and plans were devised in the workshop sessions to minimise the risks to researchers. Measures agreed included interviewing in pairs and working during daylight hours where possible.

5. Identifying the interviewer

    Decisions about the division and organisation of labour and about who interviews whom should be devolved to the community themselves. This recognises that they are the experts in their own community dynamics. It avoids a rather programmatic imposition by the researchers about the meanings of social differentiations such as age and gender to respondents and interviewers. And it allows judgements about the importance of personal networks in securing interviews and obtaining appropriate match-ups to be made on the ground.

6. Quality of data collected

    It is necessary to assert and get agreement with the commissioners of the research that employing interviewers who might be regarded as partisan appears to strengthen rather than weaken the quality and completeness of the data collected.

7. Support workshops

    It is important that ongoing support workshops are arranged throughout the period of data collection and beyond so that community researchers are supported and their work properly supervised. Also community leaders other than those directly engaged in the research should have an acknowledged role in providing a complementary sounding board to the one offered by the research supervisors.

8. Establishing commitment

    The possibility of developing collaborative work with community members depends on establishing a long-term relationship with community groups. Factors thought likely to help establish trust include demonstrating a commitment to work beyond professional boundaries; to work outside 9 to 5 hours; to contribute unpaid work of your own; to be accessible to researchers (for example giving home telephone numbers as contacts as in Oakley 1992); to make offers to contribute your expertise [e.g. in Leicester this involved 'translating' a form rich in medical jargon into plain English for the self-help group]; not to wait to be asked; and to maintain contact over a protracted time-scale.

9. The importance of providing feedback to the community

    This involves not only disseminating results widely in accessible formats (community conferences; newsletters in appropriate languages, etc.). It also means having regard to the possible consequences of revealing information about less-powerful groups to powerful decision makers where this is not in the interests of the community themselves;

providing opportunities to check the interpretation of results with community members before dissemination; involving community members in devising recommendations and demonstrating a commitment to see action taken on the basis of the results.

(2) Derby City Council / Barnardo's; Community Consultation Sinfin Estate, Derby

The second example of social action research began life as a feasibility study. The Centre for Social Action was approached by Derby City Council Economic Development Unit and Barnardo's to carry out a feasibility study for a nursery for the Sinfin Estate, Derby.

Issues for researchers arising from this project

General Points

1. The first thing the researchers did was to renegotiate the brief on the basis of our commitment to the values and processes outlined above and our knowledge both of socially excluded communities and child care. As professional researchers and community workers we are aware that child care needs do not exist in a vacuum; they are connected to other issues, such as employment/unemployment, poverty, housing policy, training. Initial enquiries showed that a feasibility study was premature and inappropriate as these connections had not been thought through or addressed. It was important that we did not collude in a token exercise to prove that a nursery was needed, just to confirm what the sponsors wanted to do anyway.

2. If Barnardo's and the city council were going to invest money on the estate it was important that the community was involved in defining the parameters of the study and asked much broader questions around needs, concerns, problems, priorities and solutions.

3. Our priority was to create community ownership of the work. Also, initial discussions with the local community development worker revealed that members of the local community had been trying to get people interested in improving the day care on the local housing estate for a number of years. By the time the feasibility study had been commissioned community involvement had dwindled. The local authorities and Barnardo's were putting together a joint funding package as part of a bid to the Single Regeneration Budget. This meant that the project was now being designed with little active community involvement and was in danger of being dominated by the requirements of its two main funders.

Learning Points

1. Only use community members as researchers when appropriate.

   Having successfully renegotiated the brief with the sponsors we then set about reawakening community interest in the project. One of the earliest conversations was around whether community members should act as researchers. The view expressed on the estate was that it was inappropriate as there were too many suspicions and divisions within the community and therefore it would not work because the information gathered would not be forthcoming or where it was would not be accurate. Also, nobody we contacted was interested in or felt confident enough to take on the role of researcher. People also said they would value having an 'authoritative outside voice' that could articulate 'the community's views' (Hadfield 1997).

2. Involve stakeholders

   Developing a baseline of professionals' concerns alongside community views meant the consultation started with what was termed an 'Orientation Report'. This report was based on a series of short interviews with the professionals who worked on the estate. It was important to gain a sense of the perceptions and concerns of these local professionals so that later they could be juxtaposed with those of the local residents collected in the main report. Putting these two perspectives together would hopefully provide a critical challenge to the agenda of the two main agencies, the city council and Barnardo's, involved in developing the project. This challenge is based on identifying the contradictions and gaps between the perspectives of professionals and members of the local community (Hadfield 1997).

3. Maintain community involvement

   The next phase fell into three parts:

   a)   Community consultation based on themes drawn from the orientation phase

   b)   Case studies of other local community based approaches to child care

   c)   Action plans based on preferred options

   What ran through all of these parts was a commitment to community involvement. At the end of parts 1 and 2 a workshop was convened and all participants invited. Regular feedback on progress was given along the way to focus group members, but this workshop was the first occasion when all the stakeholders came together. Community members were involved in checking the validity of information collected and in devising the recommendations. There were regular reports to an inter-agency group but there were only professionals on it.

4. Involve community members in devising recommendations

The purpose of the workshop was to feed back the findings and involve all the stakeholders in devising the recommendations. Community members not only articulated their support for the report, as it expressed their views, but went on to argue that they used to be involved in running child-care activities – mother and toddler, after school clubs, and holiday play schemes – before the council 'took them over'. When asked if they would like to be involved in the development of a new service a number said they would. However, training and jobs emerged as higher priorities. The recommendations that emerged from this process were to instigate a community development process that would enable community members to set up, run, and manage their own community nursery where they could get training and employment.

5. Shift the agenda

Both of the research sponsors were pleased with the results and worked hard to change their own organisations' policies and procedures, to accommodate the recommendations that they had committed themselves and their organisations to as stakeholders in the research process. Their perceptions shifted a long way in the course of the research. By the end they could see that the social action research approach was a clear way of achieving their goals of social justice and community-capacity building and sustainability. Having secured an outcome to which the community felt ownership, they formed themselves into a steering group for the new project.

6. Negotiate ongoing support

The Centre for Social Action were able to negotiate an extension to their role to support the group until a full-time community development worker was appointed. With the support of the researchers the group were involved in all the major decision making, including interviewing and appointing the community development worker. The researchers describe this process as 'protecting' the group from the various agendas of the local professionals and agencies, who became increasingly interested in what they were doing as the funding arrived.

Conclusions

The ongoing work of the Centre for Social Action is informed and improved by the experiences in this chapter. At the time of writing, researchers from the Centre are engaged in social action enquiries into a wide range of subjects including involving young people in community regeneration, community-led child care, and community safety. While the traditional and conventional research methodologies continue to dominate, the response from community members and service users reinforces the relevance and applicability of the social action approach. The slow but steady growth in the number and range of this type of research projects, nationally and internationally, is a tribute to the grit and determination shown by people on the receiving end of inappropriate and outmoded research and working practices. The demand for this approach comes from the bottom up and from professionals who side with the people who they are paid to work with. Only by researchers successfully working in partnership with community members and service users can a situation be achieved whereby research participants are not themselves estranged from the research process (Oliver 1992). Only by conducting research which is driven from the bottom up, has tangible benefits for the respondents, effects change, and provides community feedback, can the conditions for changing the social relations of research production (Oliver 1992) begin to be established. The social action research approach reaches parts that other research approaches cannot reach because it achieves a more accurate representation of service users and communities groups when evaluating services and because it involves them, wherever possible, at every stage in the process.

References

Bourdieu, P. and Passeron, J. C. (1977) *Reproduction in Education, Society and Culture*. London: Sage.

Bourne, J. and Sivananden, A. (1981) Cheerleaders and Ombudsmen. Race and Class. XX1 (4) pp 331-52

Croft, S. and Beresford, P. (1983) *From Paternalism to Participation, Involving People in Social Services*. London: Open Services Project.

Croft, S. and Beresford, P. (1993) *Getting Involved. A Practical Manual. London*: Open Services Project.

Davies, N. (1977) Dark Heart: *The Shocking Truth about Middle Britain*. London: Chatto and Windus.

Dyson, S. (1995) 'Clients-as-researchers: issues in haemoglobinopathy awareness', *Social Action*, 2(4), pp.4 -10.

Dyson, S and Goyder, E. (1994a) *Sickle Cell Anaemia: Current Carrier and Community Awareness in Leicester*. DMU Haemoglobinopathy Series, No. 1. Leicester. De Montfort University.

Dyson, S. and Goyder, E. (1994b) *Beta-thalassaemia: Current Carrier and Community Awareness in Leicester*. DMU Haemoglobinopathy Series, No 3. Leicester: De Montfort University.

Dyson S. and Harrison M. (1997) Black community members as researchers: two projects compared. Paper presented at conference: Racism and Welfare. Preston. April 1996.

Field, F. (1989) *Losing Out: The Emergence of Britain's Underclass*, London: Blackwell

Fleming, J. and Ward, D. (forthcoming) The ethics of community health needs assessment: searching for a participant centred approach. Paper presented at the Ethics and Community International Conference. Blackpool October 1995.

Fleming, J., Harrison, M., Perry, A., Purdy, D., Ward, D. (1983). 'Action Speaks Louder than Words. *Youth and Policy* 2 (3) pp 16-9.

Freire, P. (1972). *Pedagogy of the Oppressed*. Harmondsworth: Penguin.

Freire, P. (1972). *Cultural Action for Freedom*. Harmondsworth: Penguin.

Gilroy, P. (1992). *'There ain't no black in the Union Jack': the cultural politics of race and nation* . Routledge.

Hadfield, M. (1997) *Community Consultation: Power, Politics and Policies*. Nottingham: The Urban Programme Research Group.

Harrison, M. (1993) *Housing Feasibility Study on Behalf of Praxis Housing Committee*. Leicester: Centre for Social Action.

Harrison, M., Boulton, I., Abdirashid Gulaid; Mohammed Ismail, and Rhodda Saeed (1995) *Research into the Needs of the Somali Community in the City Challenge Area of Tower Hamlets*. Leicester: Centre for Social Action.

Holman, R. (1987) 'Research from the underside', *British Journal of Social Work*, 17, pp.669-83.

Kidd, R. and Kumar, K. (1994) Co-opting Freire: a critical analysis of pseudo-Feirean adult education. *Social Action*, 2(2) pp 11-8.

Mullender, A. and Ward, D. (1991). *Self-Directed Groupwork – Users Taking Action for Empowerment*. London: Whiting and Birch.

Murray, C. (1996) 'Underclass The Crisis Deepens in Lister R. (ed.) *Charles Murray and the Underclass The Developing Debate*, The Institute of Economic Affairs pp 99-135.

Oakley, A. (1981) 'Interviewing women: a contradiction in terms' in Roberts, H. (ed.) *Doing Feminist Research*. London: Routledge & Kegan Paul.

Oliver, M. (1992) 'Changing the social relations of research production', *Disability, Handicap and Society*, 7(2), pp.101-14.

Sivanandan, A. (1991) 'Black struggles against racism' in Central Council for Education and Training in Social Work (ed.) *Anti-Racist Social Work Education: Setting the Context for Change*. London: CCETSW.

Taylor, G. (1997) 'Ethical Issues in Practice: participatory social research and groups. *Groupwork* Volume 9 (2) pp.110-27.

Williams, S. (1998), Article in *The Guardian*, February 11, 1998.

Chapter 10
User involvement in large-scale research: bridging the gap between service users and service providers?

Carole Truman

Service provision in health and social welfare has commonly been informed by 'official statistics' and a variety of large-scale social surveys of populations conducted and formulated within the positivist tradition. A number of commentators have observed ways in which large-scale and official data have misrepresented, obscured, or overlooked marginalised groups in society (Graham 1993, 1995; Macfarlane 1993; Roberts 1993). There is an apparent dichotomy between those who mistrust statistics and query their status and those who confer 'canonisation' (Stanley 1996:9) – some to the point of dismissal of those who labour to show what can be done with quantitative data and how data can be improved. However, this dichotomy is not as great as first appears. Although critics of social statistics are most commonly critics of the positivist tradition, many of those working in innovative ways in quantitative approaches to research recognise the limits as well as the potential of large-scale data. Uniting the pro-numbers camp with the anti-numbers camp is a recognition that statistical data, like all forms of knowledge, are socially constructed. Thus statistics, in common with other forms of knowledge, are produced, analysed, used, and misused within a wider set of social relations. In this chapter, I want to draw upon my experience of producing social statistics in applied research settings and to develop some insights into the wider social relations which impact upon the knowledge that is produced. Central to my discussion is an exploration of those who participate in research (research respondents), those who conduct the research (the researchers), and those who require and use statistical data. Too often, the literature addresses 'the surveyed' simply as an anonymous unit within a sample where they may be normalised as passive 'respondents' or exploited 'objects' of research (Oakley 1981). I want to explore the social relations of the researched in a way which moves beyond this formulation and open up the possibilities of user-groups being involved in the creation of quantitative social data.

I begin this chapter with a short story about the life of a survey. This story serves to illustrate some of the tensions contained within the use of quantitative research.

It is now more than 10 years since I took up my first research post at a university in the north of England. I was hired as a contract researcher to explore issues relating to equal opportunities for women in paid employment. At that time, despite a growth in the number of women in paid employment, equal opportunities was a new area: it was only a minority of employers who would describe themselves as having a commitment to become 'equal opportunity employers'. There was, however, a broad interest in women's role in paid employment and the emergence of equal opportunities policies in the workplace. As a young woman at the beginning of my career, I had an obvious personal and political commitment to research of this nature. The research areas in which I became involved embraced the 'problems' for women of combining paid work alongside childcare commitments (Truman 1986a, 1986b 1992). At that time the provision of accessible childcare was a central feminist issue, and one that was being recognised as central to women's participation in the labour market. At one point, I was approached by an equal opportunities officer from a local authority who was working on a feasibility study for a children's centre or workplace nursery. The officer asked me to undertake a survey of the authority's employees to establish what the level of demand might be if a nursery were to be established. I duly undertook a postal survey of 6,000 employees and was able to provide evidence that demand for nursery places exceeded planned supply by four to one. Further, it was evident that employees at all levels and job types in the local authority might benefit from this provision. Employees also indicated that they would be prepared to pay going rates for good quality, reliable childcare. In terms of demand by employees of the local authority, the workplace nursery was clearly a viable proposition. The equal opportunities officer and I felt satisfied that our research collaboration had gone some way to help bring the workplace nursery from a plan to reality: within a year, the nursery opened to its first infants. At a local level, the research, in the form of a survey, had produced evidence that had gone some way to addressing the difficulties faced by employees who combined paid work with family commitments. As women bear the brunt of childcare responsibilities, the research might also be seen as relevant to the cause of women's equality.

Some years later, whilst working in a teaching post at another university in the same area of the north of England, I visited a student who was on placement in a local social services office. She was working with a social worker in the children and families division. They were looking into ways of generating income for social services. During our meeting, the student mentioned that she was working with a report that I had written. It transpired that it was the workplace nurseries report. This report was now being used as evidence which showed that demand for workplace nursery places far exceeded supply. However, on this occasion, the evidence was being used as a means to justify the privatisation of a proportion of places in local authority nurseries. I was told that the logic behind using data from the workplace nurseries report was that, if local authority staff showed a high level of demand for workplace nursery places, then so too might staff working for other employers. Thus a certain number of local authority nursery places could be sold to this potentially lucrative but untapped market, thereby generating income for the local authority.

My purpose in using this research story is to highlight a range of issues around the use of social research and the political context in which it may be utilised. Many of the issues which I raise might be true of any methodological approach to social research, but I would argue that there is a particular poignancy attached to the use of quantitative or survey research because of the utility and status attributed to data which are presented in a statistical form. Now, I will proceed to identify and explore some of the issues in relation to the workplace nurseries report. Specifically, I want to explore some of the issues which arise in the use, misuse, appropriation, and reappropriation of quantitative research. This requires an exploration of the social relations in which the research was carried out and an understanding of the tensions between researcher participants (who in the context of social work are often service users) and research users (who may also be service providers, policy makers or planners).

At first glance, there is nothing unusual or surprising about using a survey to generate data to establish the level of need for a new service: in this case, a workplace nursery. Indeed, although this survey was done in the 1980s, irrespective of topic, the use of this type of needs assessment has strong resonance with current concerns around accountability in the public sector. For example, Cheetham (1997) relates the importance of research as central in exploring the effectiveness of services, value for money, knowledge about impact, and the wish and need to improve services. As a piece of quantitative research, the methodology used in the survey was consistent with any textbook teaching: it was piloted and its validity assessed, it was able to reach large numbers of employees and produce data in a form that was readily digestible to its intended audience (Edwards and Talbot 1994:97). In this case, the primary intended audience were officers and members of the local authority as potential providers of the workplace nursery. At this level, the context in which the survey was done was consistent with an enlightenment model of rational knowledge generation and use.

As a survey of all current employees, the research carried with it not just the authority of methodological approach but also that of the numbers involved: this was not a sample-based survey of a few hundred employees, but a blanket survey of all 6,000 city-centre employees. There were very good reasons why both the local authority and the respondents should trust the survey to be used in the context for which it was intended. Part of this context was political since the survey and its findings were linked to the authority's wider campaign for equal opportunities. Although the concept of equal opportunities has now been linked to liberal notions of workplace equality (see, for example, Cockburn 1991), equal opportunities policies in the mid-1980s were still considered innovative and consequently met with suspicion and resistance. In contrast to political rhetoric about equal opportunities and workplace nurseries, the survey provided objective and sound knowledge, or even 'proof', that there was a case to address the needs of working parents within the local authority. The survey showed that demand for the workplace nursery places would exceed supply, thus enabling the local authority to use the research as part of a truth claim to justify the development of the nursery.

In terms of this potential outcome, those employees who had taken part in the survey had, by completing and returning their questionnaires, contributed to producing this knowledge. Working parents, and in particular working mothers, could derive benefit from the knowledge created by the survey in the progressive political context where the research was carried out. Little investment in terms of time had been required from respondents, but the potential gains were quite high since each respondent (provided he or she had a child of the appropriate age) had the potential to benefit from any nursery that was developed. In contrast to more intrusive methods of research (Finch 1984) it was difficult to anticipate any damage, harm or exploitation of research participants. As a researcher, I felt that my work had, in its own small way, functioned within an anti-discriminatory framework (Everitt *et al.*, 1992) and contributed something positive for working women with children.

The above discussion may seem too obvious and simply a reflection of the knowledge base in which we would expect local authorities to operate. As a researcher, I would have assumed that the survey had achieved its aim, had it not been for my subsequent meeting with a student some years later. However, over a short period of time the political context in which local authorities operate had changed. The public sector had been subject to 'rate capping' and consequently become more pressured by market forces and budgetary constraint. In this context, the political environment of 'knowledge' had also changed. The 'truths' about supply and demand for workplace nursery places were subject to new meaning and interpretation. Although the data within my report remained the same they portrayed not a singular truth but alternative and competing interpretations. Under the new political climate the context of the report had shifted from one which might further the interests of women to one which had the potential to cause division. The findings were open to reinterpretation as evidence or 'proof' about the potential for income generation and privatisation of nursery places. Thus a research project which had origins in the promotion of equal opportunities had become part of a political mechanism of

political change and social division. Knowledge that had been produced to
establish evidence around demand for a workplace nursery was being applied
in another context.

The local and wider political climate required social workers to explore the
financial viability of reallocating day-care nursery places to the private sector
at market rates. But this could only take place by removing nursery places from
children who had been earlier identified by social workers as having a social
need for such provision. A certain number of nursery places were to be used as
a means to raise money rather than provide an educational environment for
children in need. Parents working in the private sector who might benefit from
these 'new' places were doing so at the expense of parents (working or
otherwise) whose places had been lost.

The 'knowledge' produced by my survey was clearly not neutral or static. As a
piece of qualitative research, it carried clout – the type of clout identified by
Stanley as having 'canonical status' with those in decision-making positions.
But the process through which the knowledge was used and re-used begs
questions about whose knowledge it was. From my point of view I was being
commissioned by the local authority, so clearly the research was for them. But
since the research was about nursery provision for working parents, I had an
interest in the potential for the research also being *for* working mothers. This
identifies with the perspective offered by Kelly *et al.* 1994 who say that they
see their role as researchers as being open to the groups with whom they have
common goals and concerns. In contrast, writers like Hammersley would
contend that the role of the researcher is beyond or above politics and one
which should produce this 'objective' knowledge (Hammersley and Gomm
1996). There is no doubt that objectivity underpinned the approach to the
original research – the generation of evidence that could be interpreted as
'proof' or 'fact'. But this is a stark example of how the changes in the political
context in which the research was read fundamentally altered its meaning. (See
also Humphries (forthcoming) for a detailed discussion of these issues.) It is
futile to question the rights or wrongs of the original research. However, this
exemplar serves to expose the differential power relations between the audience
for the research and those who took part in the survey. It provides an illustration
of how 'knowledge' is shaped as much by its audience as by its content. None of
the research participants would have objected to the original survey since the
purpose for which the information and their participation were required was
clear. The respondents may have had a differential investment in the research,
with the knowledge that the findings could be put to a different use in the future
beyond its original intended purpose. Although 6,000 employees were included

in the survey, the research reflected their perspectives and interests only to the extent to which they were compatible with the interests of the local authority. Ultimately, the research belonged to the local authority, rather than the participants; it was the local authority which had the power to use the knowledge in whatever way it wanted. The creation of knowledge based upon perspectives of research participants is not the same as having the power to use knowledge. Indeed, it might be viewed that the research was not really about working parents but about the political agendas of those who had the power to use the knowledge, and that is policy makers within the local authority.

The issues which I have illustrated are central to many of the reasons why quantitative research *on* research subjects has been the focus of widespread criticism and mistrust (Oakley 1981, Stanley and Wise 1993). Within the feminist research literature this mistrust of quantitative methods has been well rehearsed almost to the point where, with a few exceptions, feminist research has become a paradigm that has rejected the gaze of survey researchers (Harding 1991, Maynard and Purvis 1994, Truman 1994). Criticisms centre on the micro-politics through which data are 'extracted' from research participants leading to their objectification (Oakley 1981). Others view the value placed in quantitative data as being far beyond the value of their content (Stanley 1996). Beyond these criticisms, quantitative data in the area of 'race' statistics have been mistrusted by those who recognise that the creation of such data has been concomitant with the creation of a 'race' problem (Ahmad and Sheldon 1993). Each of these critiques raises important questions about the social relations in which quantitative data is created and used. Quantitative data is thus positioned as serving the needs of the powerful rather than the interests of the powerless.

The creation and use of qualitative research in a policy context are not without their dangers. Ribbens and Edwards (1998:4) identify tensions between the 'traditions and requirements of public academic knowledge while remaining faithful to the experiences and accounts of research participants in private settings'. They recognise the tensions within the 'interplay of voices from "public" and "private" social worlds . . . and within and between public and private settings. Acknowledging that these tensions between the public and the private, the powerful and the powerless, are present in both quantitative and qualitative research, provides the basis for exploring the social relations of all research production.

Where research is undertaken to reflect the interests of the powerless, it usually falls within the paradigm of participatory research. Here, privilege is given to alternative forms of knowing and the creation of knowledge which reflect the interests and concerns of the less powerful (de Koning and Martin 1996, Maguire 1987, Tandon 1996). Although not exclusively, participatory research which has the involvement of research participants at its centre has commonly been of a qualitative nature. This provides the basis for dialogue, exchange, and reflexivity in identifying ways of knowing and those for whom the knowledge is intended. Within a participatory paradigm, there is a commitment to develop the means such that those who contribute towards the production of knowledge may also be empowered to benefit from the knowledge which is created. In this context, knowledge is constructed as local and situated in the context of its creation.

In the final part of this chapter, I want to explore ways of reconciling the utility of quantitative research with the dangers it may bring for marginalised groups. Whilst recognising the epistemological flaws and political dangers of quantitative 'scientific' research, it remains the case that those at the margins of society are inadequately represented in large-scale data. Alongside the dangers of the 'quantitative gaze' there are costs in the under-representation and omission of the marginalised and less powerful in quantitative research. Beyond the critical mistrust and rejection of statistics, a number of commentators have argued that statistical data could be improved in ways which better reflect the interests of marginalised groups. If statistics are powerful tools in the hands of powerful people, then there is an argument for changing the nature of the way in which social statistics are produced. A proponent of this strategy is Graham (1993, 1995) who discussing problems in methods and measurement of social diversity in official data used by policy makers, notes how 'changes in the health and social care sector have been structured that require it to attend to the needs of communities' (1995:10) whilst at the same time these communities are becoming more and more heterogeneous. She notes that whilst 'official statistics and national surveys seek to provide a comprehensive picture of the health and social circumstances of the population' (1995:11) they rely on procedures that can work against inclusiveness. This exclusion comes from criteria or categories which govern entry into official statistics and social surveys and from sampling and statistical procedures. However, it is not just the imperative of the marginalised which should drive changes in the creation of official data, but policy makers as the audience for such data should also shape this change:

'As major customers for and consumers of research, it is possible to envisage purchasers and providers arguing for changes in the official data-gathering procedures which make them more inclusive of minority groups and experiences . . . the health and social care sector could exert leverage on the measures as well as the methods used in national data gathering' (1995:16-17).

But can the creation of better quantitative and statistical data be done in a way which serves the needs of both the powerful and the powerless? In other words, (how) can quantitative data be created in a participatory way whilst also achieving a wider policy-relevance? In what ways can marginalised groups participate in this form of knowing? In the remainder of this chapter, I will describe a research study which attempted to do this. In this study I saw my role as researcher as one who potentially may bridge the gap between the knowledge requirements of policy makers and the interests of those who help to create the knowledge. The research to which I refer is a large-scale (n=1,000) health needs assessment of men who have sex with men. Unlike the workplace nurseries report which was written up as an in-house document, the health needs assessment study has appeared not only as a report in the public domain (Truman *et al.* 1995), but also in many other guises – at conferences (Truman and Gudgion 1996) and in other articles and papers (Truman 1995 and Truman forthcoming). Thus, it is not a static piece of research but has been targeted at different audiences and put to different uses. Most importantly, it has been used and re-used by the group and constituency who participated in its production.

Entering the paradigm of the powerful

The initiative for the health needs assessment came from a gay men's health group, Healthy Gay City (HGC), which as a voluntary organisation was heavily dependent upon raising funds for its survival. HGC operate mainly as potential service providers around HIV/AIDS prevention and education, but as a gay men's organisation they are also a user group. They identified that a large-scale survey of health needs might provide data which could be used to influence purchasers and fundholders. Data were needed to show what health needs existed amongst the gay and bisexual population and how those needs might be met through funded initiatives. Having identified the purpose of the survey, HGC then sought to access the technical expertise to bring the survey to fruition. My role as research director was to provide that expertise. It would have been possible for me to work to their brief, design a survey, recruit interviewers, analyse the findings, and present them with the final report. However, I was conscious that, by adopting a more participatory approach, it would be possible to empower the group so that in the process of doing the survey they could also develop research skills.

The way in which this was done was to break the research down into small stages and to involve the participation of around six of the group at each stage to discuss the objectives for that stage and to share strategies. The effect of this approach was not just to enable HGC to develop research skills, but to mean also that the survey harnessed the knowledge contained within the group itself. An example of this two-way interaction is the strategy used for sampling.

Sampling is often regarded as one of the most technical aspects of quantitative research and influenced by a strong scientific base of probability (Arber 1993). As a researcher, I could have gone away and drawn up a theoretical sampling frame and decreed that this would dictate the shape of the study. However, I wanted the group to make informed decisions about how the sampling might be achieved. This was based upon the notion of 'community' and a recognition of heterogeneity within that community. We thus devised a community sampling approach which enabled us to reach the depths and breadths of a population of men who had sex with men.

Table 1

	Face to Face	**Groups**	**Snowball**	**Pilot**
No. of Responses	421	208	271	70
% of Responses	43	21	28	7
	Those on gay scene using venues	Group leaders act as advocates for questionnaires	Survey was widely discussed through gay and non-gay venues and via groups	Respondents used to 'test' questionnaire format and question wording
	Includes those who would not voluntarily fill in self-completion questionnaires	Response rate by total group membership may be determined	Distributed by friend and associates of gay men	
	Allows validation of responses via interview team feedback	Includes 'activists'	Includes 'non-scene' men and 'non-activists'	
		Provides sound basis for 'outreach' (snowball questionnaires)		
	Face-to-Face interviews	Postal response	Postal response	Face-to-Face and postal response

Source: C. Truman, L. Keenaghan and G. Gudgion (1996) *Men Who Have Sex With Men in the North West: a Peer Regional Study* p.4. Lancaster University

As Table 1 shows, our sample was sub-divided into those who use gay venues, such as pubs, clubs, and saunas. This sample was reached by trained face-to-face interviewers who had been recruited from across the gay community. Questionnaires were also placed in venues for self-completion and postal return. Another sub-section of the sample included those who are part of gay interest groups, such as gay student societies, gay church groups, and a gay opera group. These were recruited via mail-shots and the questionnaires were returned through the post. We also generated a sizeable 'snowball' sample by asking gay and bi-sexual men to distribute the questionnaires to friends who might not otherwise be included in the survey. Other viable data were gathered at the pilot stage of the study. Through this sampling strategy, the survey was able to generate 1,000 respondents and draw upon the experiences of a diverse group of gay and bisexual men. We were able to go beyond those who socialise in the 'gay scene' and also identify certain 'hidden' groups, such as those who live in rural areas, gay men over the age of 50, as well as those under the age of 18. This extensive coverage was achieved not by drawing on textbook ideas about sampling but on the expertise contained within the gay community. As a consequence, it is probable that a more sophisticated and representative sample was achieved.

This level of involvement was achieved at each stage of the survey from design of questions through to the coding of data. The involvement of HGC was accomplished through a dialogue between them, with their knowledge of the community they wanted to research, and myself as researcher with a knowledge about the process and technical requirements of quantitative research.

It was important that the research not only reflected the gay and bisexual community but that it had credibility with research users. There were many aspects of the study that were crafted in a way which would promote its accept-ability to purchasers and fundholders (see Truman, forthcoming). Some of these were presentational and included using the university logo on the cover of the report, producing it as a university publication and giving it an ISBN number. There were academic and technical aspects, such as a theoretical justification of the choice of methods and sampling procedures and choice of statistical analysis and presentation. Indeed, my role as an academic facilitated both of these dimensions of acceptability. But acceptable findings are not always palatable findings and a professional approach did not ensure that findings would reach those in positions of power. However, the sheer weight of numbers forced the case. The fact that 1,000 gay and bisexual men responded from all corners of the regional gay community, including those that are traditionally hard to reach, added a tidal wave of weight to the research. Quite simply, a study of this detail and extent could not, at a local level, be ignored. Of course there were limits to its use – not every question was asked of every sub-group in every sexual context – but the prime purpose from the user's perspective was that a case could be made for the provision of further health education and safe-sex materials which would have a major impact.

Conclusion

Quantitative methods have been criticised for their partiality, misuse, misrepresentation and exploitation in relation to the less powerful and marginalised groups. However, unless carried out within a participatory paradigm, similar accusation could be levelled at many forms of research knowledge. I have drawn attention to the way that knowledge is always situated, located, and placed within a political context of questions around those whom it serves. Given the privileged status of quantitative data, it is imperative that the less powerful are able to shape this form of knowledge. The technical competence of researchers can enable this to happen, by working in partnership with marginalised groups, research users, and service providers. Involving the less powerful and marginalised in the creation of social statistics means that this is precisely what they might become: social statistics rather than anti-social statistics! By developing these partnerships, I hope that ultimately it might be the case that the usual disclosures that appear in quantitative research, such as 'we were unable to find *any minority group*' will no longer be defensible. As the knowledge base of the marginalised is used to inform social statistics this type of statement will become more and more unacceptable. Thus research can reflect the diversity of modern day society whilst continuing to meet the demands of policy makers and other research users.

Bibliography

Ahmad, W. and Sheldon, T. (1993) ' "Race" and Statistics' In M. Hammersley (ed.) *Social Research, Philosophy, Politics and Practice* London Sage.

Arber, S (1993) 'Designing Samples' in N. Gilbert (ed.) *Researching Social Life* London: Sage.

Cheetham, J. (1997) 'The Research Perspective' in M. Davis (ed.) *The Blackwell Companion to Social Work* Oxford. Blackwell.

Cockburn, C. (1991) *In the Way of Women: Men's Resistance to Sex Equality in Organisations* Basingstoke. Macmillan.

de Koning, K. and Martin, M. (1996) (eds.) *Participatory Research in Health: Issues and Experiences* London. Zed.

Edwards, A. and Talbot, R. (1994) *The Hard-Pressed Researcher* Harlow Longman.

Everitt, A., Hardicker, P., Littlewood, J. and Mullender, A. (1992) *Applied Research For Better Practice* BASW Macmillan.

Finch, J. (1984) 'It's Great to Have Someone to Talk to: the Ethics and Politics of interviewing Women' in C. Bell and H. Roberts (eds.) S*ocial Researching: Politics, Problems, Practice* London Routledge and Kegan Paul.

Graham, H. (1993) *Hardship and Health in Women's Lives* Hemel Hempstead Harvester Wheatsheaf.

Graham, H. (1995) 'Diversity, inequality and official data: some problems of method and measurement in Britain' *Health and Social Care in the Community* 3: 19-18.

Hammersley, M. and Gomm, R. (1996) 'Exploiting Sociology for Equality?' *Network* no. 65 May (19-20).

Harding, S. (1991) *Whose Science Whose Knowledge? Thinking From Women's Lives* Milton Keynes, Open University Press.

Humphries, B. (forthcoming) 'From Critical Thought to Emancipatory Action: Contradictory Research Goals?' in C. Truman *et al.* op. cit.

Humphries, B. and Truman, C. (1993), (eds.) *Re-thinking Social Research: Anti-discrimination in Research*, Aldershot Avebury.

Kelly, L., Burton, S., and Regan, L. (1994) 'Researching Women's Lives, or Studying Women's Oppression?' in M. Maynard and J. Purvis (eds.) op. cit.

Macfarlane, A. (1993) 'Official Statistics and Women's Health and Illness' in H. Roberts (ed.) op. cit.

Maguire, P. (1987) *Doing Participatory Research: A Feminist Approach* University of Massachusetts.

Maynard, M. and Purvis, J. (1994) (eds.) *Researching Women's Lives From a Feminist Perspective* London Taylor and Francis.

Oakley, A. (1981) 'Interviewing Women: a contradiction in terms?' in H. Roberts (ed.) *Doing Feminist Research* London Routledge and Kegan Paul.

Ribbens, J. and Edwards, R. (1998) (eds.) *Feminist Dilemmas in Qualitative Research: Public Knowledge and Private Lives* London Sage.

Roberts, H. (1993) ed. *Women's Health Counts* London Routledge.

Stanley, L (1996) *Sex Surveyed 1949-94* London Taylor and Francis.

Stanley, L. and Wise, S. (1993) *Breaking Out Again* London Routledge.

Tandon, R. (1996) 'An Historical Theoretical Perspective to PR' In K. de Koning and M. Martin op.cit.

Truman, C. (1986a) *Overcoming the Career Break – A Positive Approach* Manpower Services Commission Sheffield.

Truman, C. (1986b) *Survey of the Childcare Requirements of City Centre Employees of Manchester City Council* Manchester UMIST.

Truman, C. (1992) 'Demographic Changes and New Opportunities for Women: The case of employers' Career Break Schemes' in *Women and Working Lives: Divisions and Change* S. Arber and N. Gilbert (eds.) London Macmillan.

Truman, C. (1994) 'Feminist Challenges to Traditional Research: have they gone far enough?' in Humphries and Truman op.cit.

Truman C. (forthcoming) 'New Social Movements and Social Research' in C. Truman *et al.* (eds.)

Truman, C. and Gudgion, G. (1996) 'Community-Based Research Partnerships – A View From the Bridge' Paper presented to the HIV Project Building Bridges Conference, Institute of Education, London, March.

Truman, C. Humphries B. and Mertens, D. (forthcoming) *Research In An Unequal World* London Falmer Press / UCL.

Truman, C. Keenaghan, L. and Gudgion, G (1996) *Men Who Have Sex With Men in the North West: A Peer-Led Needs Assessment* (Lancaster University / Healthy Gay Manchester).

Chapter 11
The politics of joint agency-university research

Louise Brown and Lisa Loveridge

This chapter considers the context within which joint agency-university research takes place; the issues that arise within the research process and the factors that can lead to a successful collaborative relationship. It describes some of the advantages and disadvantages and discusses the requirements for successful collaboration. The information is based upon the experiences of the authors, one agency-based, one university-based, together with data from a survey of both agency and university researchers. The major part of the experience drawn upon relates to collaborative work between university departments and local authority social service departments. Here, the term 'agency' refers to those services commissioned and provided in the statutory and voluntary sectors.

When we talk about research into social work practice we are mainly referring to evaluative research that is linked in with an agency's interest in the design, development, and delivery of services. In such an applied setting very little 'pure' research will be found.

The desire to bridge the gap between research and social work practice remains. The Department of Health has invested in various projects which attempt to address this, including *Messages From Research* (DoH,1995). Yet despite the fragile nature of the relationship between research and practice the requirement to demonstrate '*value for money*', '*efficiency*' and '*effectiveness*' seems to have kept evaluative research alive. The use of research by senior managers and policy makers in social work may in fact be healthier than links further down the organisation. Such terms almost seem out of date in a culture that now identifies 'evidence based' practice as its goal and it is possible that the emergence of this concept in social work might actively assist in the attempts to integrate research and practice.

The increasing appearance and use of the phrase 'evidence-based practice' within the field of social work are relatively recent although not a new concept to those whose business is conducting and disseminating research in social work. Taken from health, the term implies a move towards basing the planning and development of services upon a more rigorous and sound research base than previously occurred. It presents a challenge to researchers to undertake reliable research that can produce 'evidence' and the challenge for agencies will be in getting their hands on this 'evidence' in a format which they can digest and absorb. Health studies have shown that there remains a failure to put research findings into practice and that the equivalent grass roots practitioners, such as GPs, still use tried and tested remedies rather than evidence-based practice (Oxman 1995, Campbell *et al.*, 1998).

Whilst few social workers would disagree with the need to evaluate the effectiveness of social work services and the use of research to inform their practice, in reality, few would be able to identify one piece of research that had directly informed the decisions or judgements that they make. The reasons for failing to get research findings into practice are many and varied including: the difficulties of accessing research; lack of time to read and absorb studies and reflect upon the implications for practice; a culture that does little to encourage and support such activities; a lack of skills to critically assess the validity of a study; and not least a dearth of reliable and valid research into social work effectiveness. It is hoped and intended that the establishment of a centre for evidence-based social services may be able to exert some influence over these difficulties.

The low status of social work theory and research among practitioners, especially in the area of services for adults, also contributes to this situation. These tensions between research and practice have been discussed in depth by Hammersley (1995), and although a study by Macdonald *et al.* (1992) reviewing the research on social work effectiveness concludes that the overall picture is less bleak than in previous decades, social work still has a long way to go before the gaps in our knowledge have been filled and the findings of such studies become rooted in practice.

Agencies and universities have historically worked together to train social work practitioners; disseminate research findings; and undertake research for the agency, or studies in which a social services department becomes the fieldwork site in a university-based project. For those local authorities who have traditionally developed links with universities or educational institutions and have an established research culture, the challenge to move towards evidence-based practice may be easier. For those who have over the years seen their own research capacity dwindle and the gulf between research and practice widen, the challenge may be greater, both financially and conceptually. Whilst collaborative research between agencies and universities is not new, the repackaging of evaluation and effectiveness studies into evidence-based social work should ensure that the future for collaborative working looks brighter.

An examination of the studies published in *Social Services Research* between 1991 and 1996 indicates that there was an overall reduction in research activity within local authorities, the voluntary sector, and universities in the UK.

Table 11.1

Percentage of research that is collaborative

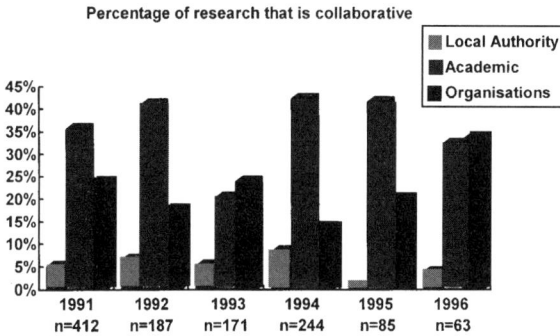

	Local Authority
	Academic
	Organisations

45%
40%
35%
30%
25%
20%
15%
10%
5%
0%

| 1991 | 1992 | 1993 | 1994 | 1995 | 1996 |
| n=412 | n=187 | n=171 | n=244 | n=85 | n=63 |

n = the total number of UK research projects listed in that year

The table indicates a trend developing in the early 1990s in the amount of research being undertaken. For example, the 1991 *SSR* listed 412 projects (the largest ever published in the review according to Martin Willis in the editorial), compared with 63 in 1996. However, the proportion of collaborative research remained relatively constant. There are a number of possible explanations for this: agencies have been forced to cut back on in-house research facilities; the importance and status of research may have dropped; funding for research may have become more difficult to secure, or funders may be moving towards supporting fewer numbers of bigger projects. This last-mentioned reason could be an early indication that social work research is moving towards a more-scientific, evidence-based approach.

There are pockets of collaborative work, for example in 1991 Sheffield Family and Community Services Department listed 36 research projects (in itself one of the largest entries for a local authority), of which 10 involved a variety of academic institutions. Such situations may arise where there is a strong research culture or history of research, where an organisation gives priority to staff development and therefore funds higher degrees, or where senior managers in an organisation give priority to research. Once good collaborative relationships have developed and there is trust, the likelihood of more joint work is increased.

The information which follows is based upon responses to a questionnaire and on the experiences of the authors. A questionnaire was sent to all 50 people whose research was listed in the 1996 no. 2 issue of *SSR* and for whom a postal address could be obtained. This was the most recent issue available and although not a random sample of the research undertaken in that year it does

161

not have any obvious biases. Sixteen responses were received (a response rate of 32%) from seven agency researchers and nine based in universities. A total of nine had no experience of non-collaborative work, two had no experience of collaborative research, and five had participated in both.

To those who have established relationships, the advantages of collaborative working between agencies and universities seem obvious. For agencies it might offer practical benefits such as access to research skills, perhaps library and search facilities, and postgraduate training opportunities for staff. The university can offer a means of taking research questions and projects forward in a way that is deemed to add credibility to any findings produced. This is especially important where the area of practice to be researched is sensitive and the objectivity of a university-based researcher might allow for greater access into difficult research areas and make staff less suspicious of the process and findings. The results may be received differently and in a way which allows for better implementation.

For universities facing increasingly tight funding arrangements linked to their research activities, the advantages are clear. Their funders are looking more and more for partnership arrangements, a demonstration that the research is sufficiently linked to policy and practice trends and that it takes account of the needs and views of service users and their carers. Many of the large grant-making bodies have made partnerships a prerequisite for the application. For example, the National Lottery Charities Board Health and Social Research Programme, states 'We will only fund research based in university departments and research centres where there is collaboration with, and the application is submitted by, a charity or voluntary organisation.'

In this context and within the area of social work practice, collaborative arrangements for research become increasingly important. Information gathered from our survey suggests that university researchers benefit from and value the expertise that they can find within the agency. They experience better and easier access to management information and service users and practitioners. In turn the project design and sample are strengthened. Where service users are involved, their agenda is enabled to come to the fore. Some reported that a practice perspective lends itself to producing results that are more focused and therefore more useful. It was felt that collaborative research could contribute to anti-discriminatory practice by enabling researchers to share the perspectives of others and by using research to raise the profile of some issues within the media and among practitioners.

For both agencies and universities collaborative arrangements may legitimise and lend credibility to research. The ways in which they might come together will differ, depending upon the reason for the links. For example, if it is to undertake a new piece of research the agency might commission the university and fund the research itself. Alternatively, a university may approach one or a number of agencies for access to fieldwork sites, take the agencies as partners in the project, and make a joint application to a funder. Other formal or informal relationships might exist between agencies and university departments, such as agencies funding a post within a university. Research projects might then be negotiated jointly and undertaken in partnership. Each arrangement encompasses its own set of difficulties and issues which have to be worked through.

The respondents did identify some disadvantages and stated that commissioning independent research was expensive. Whereas in the past it may have been possible for academics to go into an agency to research an aspect of practice as part of their paid employment, the reality of the current funding situation in universities means many research centres are run as small businesses, dependent upon external grants to survive. Not only does research need to be costed to replace teaching time lost to it, but budgets must also include university overheads and infrastructure and salary costings. At a time when agencies have faced many years of cuts, with the likelihood that these will continue, it seems increasingly difficult to justify expenditure for research.

Joint working can be time consuming as there are a number of stakeholders with whom the project must be negotiated and agreed. Developing joint working arrangements can also take time and working with two organisations can mean a doubling of bureaucracy! One of the greatest differences in expectations between agencies and university researchers can be over the timescale for completing and turning a project around. Reflecting their different agendas, a social services department may require information about a service quickly in order to decide on future funding whereas a researcher will wish to have sufficient time to carry out the project to his or her design. Where new services are being evaluated with a view to further funding or expansion into mainstream practice, decisions will inevitably need to be taken early for budgetary reasons. The researcher may therefore have to compromise on his or her design and may elect a process-orientated approach which looks at the goals, expectations, and needs of the target population as opposed to an impact study that would require additional information about outcome and causality. The former type of study is likely to cost less and fall short of the methodological standards required to promote its findings as 'evidence'. This may make it less appealing to researchers and begins to open up the debate about the difference between research and consultancy. This may offer a further explanation for the decline in the number of research projects being undertaken in social service departments.

Quite often an agency will be commissioning the work as part of a development process or to obtain information upon which to base decisions or develop a strategy. Few agencies will commission research for their general interest. Whether the work is defined as 'applied research' or consultancy will often depend upon its purpose. It will be of no interest to the agency how it is defined, but this may be important to the university who may have to charge VAT on consultancy. The university will want the research grant and the intellectual property rights (in order to publish from the study) to contribute towards their next research assessment exercise. An agency may refer to a project as research but may in fact be asking the research team to draw conclusions and make recommendations on the basis of the findings. The researchers may feel that this is not part of their role. Hence the 'outputs' from the project need to be discussed, clarified, and agreed in advance in a written contract.

Despite often sharing interests in subject areas, for example the impact of alcohol and drug misuse on children and families, agencies and universities clearly have different agendas and often speak a different language. In the survey, individuals from both the agencies and universities complained about the use of jargon and academic language.

The different agendas that arise within collaborative research pose enormous potential problems to overcome, not least in relation to defining the research questions and project design. Where a university is being commissioned by an agency they do not have equal power and control over the research project. In circumstances where the agency and university construct a joint proposal and secure external funding, i.e. one is not commissioning the other, the potential for difficulties to arise remains great, although the power should be more even.

The differing agendas become more apparent as projects progress. Initially an interest is shared and the aims of a project might easily be expressed and agreed. Specifying the objectives by which the aims will be achieved starts to highlight differences in approach and emphasis. Universities want to be able to publish papers in journals based upon their research. Therefore, the methodology they choose needs to be reliable and they will often want the project design to be robust enough for the results to be generalisable outside of the specific fieldwork sites. Any published research will be susceptible to the scrutiny and comments of other academics and will need to stand up to peer review.

The specific questions that the research will address may well differ and create a tension within the research process. The university might wish to address a series of questions that relate to a much wider policy debate that lies outside the interests of the agency. For example, collaboration between health and social services is high on the national and local agenda. The university may pose questions that seek to analyse the ways in which national policy has been interpreted and achieved. A social services department might want to understand more about the services that they are providing in this area (*process*). The university might want to focus upon the 'impact' of changes in service (*outcomes*), whilst the local authority might only want to focus on a hospitals discharge process and the implications for nursing home beds. The local authority might wish the research to indicate how well they are doing, whilst the university might have a hypothesis which suggests that policies are not working in this area in relation to their objectives. Each set of questions requires different types of information to be gathered and a different project design. Such differences, or 'pluralist perspectives' as Cheetham *et al.* (1992) put it, highlight the politics of collaborative research 'In almost every study, difficult choices must be made about what can be examined and few single studies can do justice to all the questions of conflicting perspectives'.

Therefore, negotiating and agreeing the research brief can be fraught with difficulties. The specific questions to be addressed differ not only between university and agency but between individuals *within* the agency. A team manager or social worker will have a different interest from a senior manager whose agenda will be different to that of a service user; while a practitioner who seeks funding from his or her employer for a higher degree will have to bend to the ideas of both the employer and academic supervisor. Either way, the research questions will determine the shape and scope of the project and the methodology will be designed around the questions to be answered.

It would be usual for the researchers to design the method of data collection and analysis, since this is their area of expertise. The agency will know, or should know, what information is already routinely collected and available. The skill in this part of the process is in designing a methodology that produces good quality information but that is not too difficult for an agency to implement. The randomised control trial, the so-called gold-standard of methods, even if it were appropriate may prove too difficult to implement. This raises the classic ethical issue of withholding a service or treatment from an individual. However, some local authority social service departments, having recognised the consequences and difficulties of obtaining *evidence* are becoming more open to this more rigorous type of research request.

Achieving a big enough sample size might mean practitioners have to gather data for prolonged periods of time, which will often not be acceptable and will result in poor-quality data. Researchers and practitioners will need to agree what information is readily accessible and at what point service users should be made aware of a study and their consent sought for their details to be included. This threshold may differ between university and agency, where the latter are more accountable in this respect. Where service users' and carers' views are to be recorded the process for achieving permission can appear lengthy and frustrating to a researcher who is ready and waiting.

In many cases the scale and scope of a project will be determined largely by the budget. For example, a question around measuring the impact of a new service on the health of older people could result in a project design which uses tried and tested quality of life and health scales with a 12 month follow-up built in. This would be significantly more costly than a design that used client-satisfaction-type questionnaires to determine 'impact'. The researchers need to be prepared to accept that the methodology will ultimately depend upon a number of factors to do with the power and control of certain individuals and the budget, and not solely upon the questions to be answered.

In defining the methodology the issue of involving service users and their carers in the research needs addressing. In many ways the decision is a political one – to what extent should service users and carers have a say in determining the research agenda, the questions to be asked, the way data is gathered and who does it? One view is that research should be user led and that this means moving beyond consulting with users but enabling them to undertake the research them-selves. Their agendas will undoubtedly differ and the issue raises many questions about power and control. Users and carers have little control over the funding of research and similarly little power to change the process. This is a debate that has not fully surfaced but is likely to do so in the near future as planners are required to pay more attention towards user and carer views. Greater involvement of service users in the research process might in fact generate better quality data through improved access to users and carers. Access to information is a crucial part of the research, and difficulties often demonstrate the different levels of commitment to the research within the agency.

Universities and agencies have very different requirements, which will result in different types of outputs for very different audiences. Universities will want to publish papers in academic and practice journals, which may require more detail on the policy context of the research. Such papers will have a different focus and may draw upon different aspects of the findings. For agencies the results need to be focused on more immediate practice or policy issues. Findings will need to be fed back to those with a policy development brief and should be disseminated in a manner which is accessible to service users (Everitt 1992).

Establishing a mutual interest and commitment to a topic is the easy part of any collaborative relationship. Where this relationship and process have already been tried and tested and found to be successful, trust will have been obtained and future projects are likely to flow. Where new relationships are being formed the potential for tripping up is great as expectations will differ from the start. Agencies need to be educated about the complicated research process, in relation to what it costs, how long it takes and what it involves. It is a relationship that requires careful preparation if it is to achieve its aims.

The use of a written contract is crucial to establishing a good collaborative relationship and is useful in clarifying expectations. The contract needs to be specific about timescales, deadlines, costs, and the different outcomes and outputs that will emerge. It is a useful vehicle for clarifying the aims and more importantly the specific objectives of a project. The research design must be clearly stated and a management structure put into place. For the university the contract needs to cover the issue of who owns the data, publication rights, and what happens to the proceeds from the sale of any reports. Where contracts are not well defined and organisations rely upon informal relationships the project can feel and become very fragile. The potential for individuals to make assumptions about what the research is going to cover and provide at the end of the day is enormous.

Most projects that involve different organisations will need steering. The agency will wish to ensure that the end results are useful for them and that the timescales are adhered to, and the researchers may need help with accessing information at different points. All need to own the project. Where one organisation loses interest part-way through, the process can suddenly become much more difficult to move on, specific agendas can start to dominate and the overall results may be skewed.

The commitment required in time and motivation is great. Agencies are often unaware of the importance of maintaining their level of enthusiasm. Individuals involved in the research need certain personal and professional skills for this to work well. All need to be flexible at certain times, honest all of the time, and respect the position of the relative parties. In the survey that we carried out, 'trust' was identified by a number of researchers and agency representatives as being a crucial component in a successful collaborative relationship. The degree of diplomacy and negotiating skills often called upon would make any individual particularly well qualified for a job with the UN.

Most respondents were positive about collaborative research whilst recognising the difficulties that are inherent within it. It was felt that the clarity which comes from contracts and the interpersonal qualities such as openness, flexibility, goodwill, honesty, respect, and keeping partners informed are important in making collaborative research work.

Whilst recognising the difficulties in undertaking collaborative research, it is evidently of considerable value to practitioners and academics alike. Judging by the stability of the data from SSR, it is likely to continue to play an important part in the development of practice.

References

Campbell, N.C. Thain, J. Deans, H.G. Ritchie, L.D. and Rawles, J.M. (1998) Secondary prevention in coronary heart disease: baseline survey of provision in general practice. *BMJ* 1998; 316:1430-4.

Cheetham, J. Fuller, R. McIvor, G. and Petch A. (1992) *Evaluating Social Work Effectiveness*. Open University Press.

Department of Health (1995) *Child Protection: Messages From Research. Studies in Child Protection*. HMSO, London.

Everitt, A. Hardiker, P. Littlewood, J. and Mullender A. (1995) *Applied Research For Better Practice*. Macmillan, London.

Hammersley, M. (1995). *The Politics of Social Research*. Sage Publications Ltd London.

Macdonald, G. Sheldon, B. and Gillespie, J. (1992) 'Contemporary Studies of the Effectiveness of Social Work'. *British Journal of Social Work*, 22(6). pp 615-43

National Lottery Charities Board (1998) *Health and Social Research Application Pack*.

Oxman, A. (1995). No Magic Bullets. *Canadian Medical Association Journal*. 153, pp 1423-31.

Social Services Research (1991) No. 1 Department of Social Policy and Social Work University of Birmingham.

Social Services Research (1992) No. 2 Department of Social Policy and Social Work University of Birmingham.

Social Services Research (1993) No. 3 Department of Social Policy and Social Work University of Birmingham.

Social Services Research (1994) No. 3 Department of Social Policy and Social Work University of Birmingham.

Social Services Research (1995) No. 3 Department of Social Policy and Social Work University of Birmingham.

Social Services Research (1996) No. 2 Department of Social Policy and Social Work University of Birmingham.

Lisa would like to thank Helen Harris and Ann Davis at Birmingham University for their assistance and her partner Chris Murphy for his support.

Chapter 12
Practitioner research in community care
– personalising the political

Helen Gorman

Introduction

The maintenance of the equilibrium between the personal and the political is fundamental to our social science as well as to the praxis of our social life. Paul Halmos in *The Personal and the Political* (1978)

Practitioner researchers often need help to construct their research map. This chapter draws on secondary data, namely Masters dissertations from the MSc in Collaborative Community Care at the University of Central England 1992-7 and incorporates the experiences of a tutor on that programme who mentored some of the students during their research. Qualitative approaches to practitioner research are discussed, drawing on a feminist epistemology which acknowledges that value neutrality is imperfect in the context of the 'community care revolution' of the 1990s: a contested area of both policy and practice. The growth of practitioner research in health and social care, often associated with taught Masters programmes, has opened up the field of research to many practitioners who may have fought shy of 'traditional' academic research degrees, considering them too abstruse or irrelevant to everyday practice. The advantages of doing practitioner research based on current practice and utilised by employer agencies (and, hopefully, the client population) need to be balanced against the difficulties arising from being immersed in the pressures of undertaking time-limited research early into the course, and by being so close to the focus of the research. Practitioner researchers undertaking qualitative research for higher degrees can experience a 'policy is us' paradigm: a recognition that during this process of the research small 'p' and large 'P' political issues can arise that require managing oneself in territory which may be familiar yet, in research terms, still uncharted. To experience practitioner research within an interpretivist paradigm means recognising who you are, as researcher, in relation to others, with full account being taken of the history of the inquiry process itself.

Contextualising practitioner research in community care

Halmos's statement, reminds us of a time when it was believed that 'the state' had a monopoly on social concerns and the means of remedying them. His seminal text *The Personal and The Political* (1978) was a statement about balance, about recognising and managing a dichotomy in social work practice, and balancing a desire to help those in need with a fear that, by so doing, support is being given to a system which should itself be changed. As the millennium becomes a reality, the notions of the personal and the political have taken on a similar but different resonance; one fuelled by economic changes, the growth of the 'consumer movement', and an emergent 'new citizenship' and 'new welfare'. This has been particularly significant in the fields of health and social care, where the notions of 'the state mediated professional' (Johnson 1972) have been replaced by changing occupational roles and dynamic processes of occupational formations. The 'political' remains important, but it has taken on different formulations. For the practitioner researcher working in community care the 'community care revolution' of the 1990s brought many changes to practitioner roles in health and social care. The move away from the public service work ethic to the market approach to welfare has affected the work orientation of health and welfare staff (McGrath 1996, Gorman 1996). These changes have affected the role of social workers in community care who, when acting as care managers, intervene in 'the market' on a regular basis. Doing research at the cutting edge of practice in community care requires an understanding of how the personal relates to the political, not as an esoteric exercise but as an everyday reality.

It is possible to reify the politics of community care at a theoretical level, but that is not the intention of this chapter which takes an approach that practice theory is grounded in the rationalisations of individuals and groups as part of an iterative process, for

> *. . . just as different groups participate to varying degrees in the formulation of community care policy, so they contribute to the practice of this policy. Just as the 'political' is not something 'out there' but a part of our own rationalisations manifest in our everyday courses of action, so the economic is an aspect of everyday life which influences and constrains actions, in turn those actions contribute to the official rationality* (Simms 1989).

How people feel and what they learn in the *process* of the research as well as the research outcomes are intrinsically part of the policy formation. Some authors, for example Ely *et al.* (1991), have seen this as an intensely personal, recursive process. The personalising of the political is bound up with power (Freire 1972): it is impossible to separate knowledge generated throughout the research process from dimensions of power. Possibilities of meaning are pre-empted through the social and institutional position from which the discourse comes, for as Ball (1990) comments, 'policies are statements about practice, the way things could or should be, they derive from statements about the world, about the way things are'.

Power dimensions bind the political with the practice. The small 'p' political may be about how people relate to each other in the work which impacts upon the personal. The larger 'P', the wider political focus, may refer to sensitivity about the research project in terms of the topic area or the timing of the intervention in a turbulent environment (Perlmutter and Trist 1986). How the research is formulated, carried out, written up and disseminated are political acts which may be received differently by various people at certain times according to their large 'P' values. The very real small 'p' and large 'P' political issues generated by practitioner research demand rigour and transparency in data selection and analysis. Critics taking a positivist approach to research may seek to dismiss qualitative practitioner research as lacking in reliability and validity, and it is the job of the researcher to tackle these criticisms (whilst emphasising that no research in the social sciences is without methodological critique). Researchers should be able, and need, to set out clearly the interactions that have occurred between themselves and their methodologies in the chosen context. Their accounts should be trustworthy and authentic (Lincoln and Guba 1985), for this will impact on how the outcomes of the research are received.

It can be argued that the growth in the use of quasi-statistics as 'the' evidence when used to support one policy option or approach over another, has led to some mistrust of research among practitioners and managers in health and welfare agencies. This, together with the functional 'flavour of the month' research culture, has not necessarily led to the intended outcomes for community care users. An understanding that different research perspectives make different kinds of knowledge claims is fundamental to the creation of the research discourse and to the dissemination of project findings. Qualitative practitioner research can make certain claims and has numerous strengths: it implies a direct concern with experience as it is lived and an understanding of that experience in context. It is powered by a group of disciplined procedures that must be studied, practised, learned and relearned (Ely *et al.* 1991).

Ethnographic practitioner research relies heavily upon the researcher as an instrument. A feminist epistemology acknowledges that relationships established between a researcher and fieldwork can influence the development of research accounts and therefore ultimately affect the formulation of theory

(Oakley 1981, Finch 1984). From the very early stages of 'hunches' which develop into research proposals, through to the dissemination of findings, an acknowledgement of tacit knowledge is an essential part of the research process.

The practitioner researcher undertaking qualitative research for a Masters degree has a bounded task. The work has to be possible within a given time frame and is usually completed whilst in full-time work and when there are often family responsibilities and agency expectations about the research's utility. Experience of working on the University of Central England's Collaborative Community Care Masters degree has shown that practitioners and managers who succeed on the course are keen to improve community care practice and policy. Practitioner research is distinctive in that 'it makes connections between what is happening and what could happen' (Broad and Fletcher 1993) and hence how practice can be improved. In qualitative practitioner research there is an element of personal reflexivity in that the research relates to the practitioner's own identity and the topic chosen derives from personal concerns about, for example, the changing nature of the social worker's role in community care or the help available to carers in the community. These are topics that can be close to the practitioner researcher's heart and mind as being worthy of investigation, involving an engagement with and an acknowledgement of personal history. A reflective approach can be significant at this early stage of the research because the researcher has an autobiography marked by significations of gender, ethnicity, sexuality, and class which affects the form and outcomes of the research (Scott and Usher 1996).

Stares (1987) suggests that 'thinking units' for the analysis of qualitative data can be centred around elements in the total intervention such as *conditions, interaction amongst the actors, strategies, tactics, and consequences*. These categories are useful in considering empirical examples of practitioner research into community care and are used here to inform the analysis of research stages; from the decision about research topic, the creation of a protocol, access to data sources, gathering data, analysing it, writing up the research, and disseminating the findings. Each stage of this process requires engagement with the political and the way such political elements are configured can take everyone by surprise. What is important is that elements are managed within an ethical framework, although such a statement has to be modified by an acknowledgement that all research, including qualitative research, is inherently value laden. A recognition of this throughout all the stages of the research process can assist the researcher to understand that undertaking qualitative research can indeed be part of a process of both personal and professional growth and transformation.

Conditions – formulating the research topic and getting access

The beginning of the research process can be fraught with anxiety. The formulation of a research topic and the necessity to take on the role of *researcher* as well as or instead of *practitioner* can be difficult to manage [see Broad and Fletcher (1993) on this important point, ed.]. Pertinent observations that may be made are: Is it possible to manage a duality of roles? Will relationships with one's colleagues and clients ever be the same? A recognition of the potential for a change in relationships and how this might impact on work roles and tasks may lead the researcher to consider a different emphasis in the research focus. An understanding that a research topic is likely to touch the personal and the social is an important first hurdle, for

> *. . . seeing research as social practice forces us to recognise certain things. First, that research is not a matter of applying a set of transcendental methods or of following an algorithmic procedure. Rather it is a set of activities legitimated by a relevant community – that is one of the reasons why it is social* (Scott and Usher 1996).

Formulating the research question is in itself a political act (Wilson 1996). It can bring to the fore issues with which the researcher identifies at a personal level. It also relates to the *person as the professional* and in turn how it connects with the community of the research. Gaining access to that community to legitimate the project may be problematical. Empirical evidence from research students indicates that individuals in a position of power within work organisations can actively assist or actively block access to research. This perhaps can be understood in a climate where practice has at times become over-researched, with agencies bombarded by a range of people from those doing undergraduate work to high profile, and research agencies requesting access to research a particular intervention. It may be realistic to acknowledge that access can be difficult, particularly if the researcher is not known to that agency or has little currency of exchange. The problems research students experience in gaining access can vary in their type. In some cases colleagues and managers have actively blocked access on the premise that 'this work has already been done' or 'isn't needed' when on further investigation it has been apparent that this was about workplace jealousy or guarding positions in the hierarchy. Gaining access can often be the research student's first tussle with the political impact of investigating workplace practice and policy. Its importance cannot be overestimated, and early focused work by the practitioner researcher, tutor, and agency is vital for enabling, and then sustaining, access.

This is particularly relevant to interdisciplinary research into community care. One student from a social work background who was researching into services received by elderly people found difficulty in obtaining a sample through local clinics. She comments:

In general, provider agencies were able to give more help than pur-chasers, but overall staff were trusting and understanding of the purpose of the research. One GP refused to co-operate, believing the research to be an audit. This perhaps reflects an attitude towards current health service managerial practices. Access can be affected by many attitudinal factors which mirror the problems existing in collaborative initiatives.

Gaining access to respondents may bring to the fore macro-political issues that require sensitive handling and the development of trust in the relationships between researcher and researched. One practitioner researcher writes:

It was not easy to gain access to . . . communities. I had to have a feeling for cultural differences, for example as a Christian interviewing Muslims who were at war with Christians in their own country . . . I had to establish trust with their representative and the interpreter.

However, students often come to the research as 'known' people within the agencies they are researching; this can have benefits and disadvantages. Even if you are known to colleagues some negotiation may be necessary to gain access to a particular community. For example, in researching into residential care a social services manager comments:

A preliminary meeting with the residential staff group was set up to consider the matter of interviewing residents . . . they were concerned that residents may experience unacceptable levels of anxiety.

Access can require careful negotiating and involve the political and personal lives of others who become part of the research process. In mentoring students it may be necessary to advise them to consider other options and other approaches.

An awareness of their difference in researching undervalued groups (Wilkes 1981) is a significant issue which caused one practitioner researcher to recon-sider her strategy:

On reflection I would not do this type of study again, I would accept the advice of facilitators and those more experienced in the field of research and do the study in an area of easier access to a sample frame.

Even damage limitation can be a learning experience! The tutor has a part to play in encouraging practitioner researchers to maintain confidence in themselves and to move forward to complete the work after setbacks which could not have been entirely anticipated.

Interaction amongst actors – gathering data and data analysis

For some researchers investigating their own communities the personal and the political are as one:

> *As a black woman researcher, working specifically with . . ., I was constantly faced with real dilemmas in maintaining a balance between being a professional researcher and being myself . . . issues I struggled with were real in terms of being aware that I had open access to and interaction with people who had trust in me . . . this conscious thought made me reflective of being black in terms of a feminist perspective.*

Being a member of a particular agency can be helpful or otherwise in gaining access to research subjects. One researcher found that it was helpful to state that he represented a particular organisation when he sent out his initial contact letters.

> *The aims of the research were outlined in a letter sent to the respondents . . . the letter was written on . . . notepaper and identified the interviewer, interpreter and gave details of the research . . . the letter possibly more than any other factor accounted for the confidence with which respondents divulged a great deal of information.*

The timing of a research project can affect the outcome: often policy changes within agencies mean that re-negotiation has to take place or elements of the research project may need to be reconsidered. Such issues, even if they are outside the control of the researcher, can cause anxiety.

> *I encountered the difficulty that . . . was no longer able to participate in the research. Following the initial disappointment at the decision made by the agency, I went through a process of reflection as to why that decision had been taken. On consultation with the particular agency I was informed that the decision was based on internal staffing problems which had a dramatic effect on staff esteem and morale.*

When this type of situation occurs the researcher needs time to reflect and to consider alternatives. This may require adjustments to the research plan and perhaps the need to explore other data collection sites. This type of experience can be included as part of the research critique, often adding substance and interest to the finished work.

These comments show how the research act can be interpreted as political in its context, at times fusing the professional with the personal. Similarly, in researching health and social care services for a minority group one researcher found that:

Information obtained from service users appeared to reflect the dangers of reinforcing stigmatisation, discrimination, exploitation and oppression by service providers illustrated by one [respondent] saying to me 'my needs are the same as yours, how dare you ask me, I go to the hospital same as anyone else when I'm ill'.

The realisation that by engaging in researching others one might be continuing a form of oppression amongst stigmatised groups is a steep learning curve; a change in methodological approach and a clearer definition of the research task may ease the way towards a more manageable project. Power dynamics can shift; at times the researcher may appear to be in a powerful position, at others the researched may be identified as powerful. These dynamics often reflect the learning process, particularly in a learning environment in which the politics of difference are discussed and worked with over a period of time (Gorman *et al.* 1996). The relationships between the researcher and interviewees can also reflect power dimensions in the workplace. One researcher found that:

Interviews are either limited or helped by the interviewer's own sex, appearance, background, skin colour and accent (Oppenheim 1992) and related to this is the issue of power. The researcher interviewed senior managers who by reason of their role have authority over the researcher and this may have affected their responses. As a black woman of working class background the researcher was conscious of these issues and how they may have affected the outcome of the interviews.

Sometimes conscious or unconscious decisions are taken either to include or exclude data from the analysis and data definitions and data collection take account of the researcher's own personal constructs [also see Harris and Paylor's earlier chapter on the related point of 'essentialism' ed.]. In one project into residential care for mentally ill people the researcher states:

The project represented an area of professional interest that the author wished to see debated more widely. Statements critical of the residential services may have been unknowingly censored and bias may have been operating in relation to the data selected for inclusion in this study.

In such a context an epistemology is required which acknowledges that fieldwork relations and contexts can influence research accounts. Rigour in making decisions about data inclusion and exclusion assists in realising a need to make such analytic decisions as open and transparent as possible. The validity of the account affects how it is received by the target audience, which may be influential in policy implementation. An acknowledgement of the fusion of the personal with the political is too often underplayed in data analysis, leading to criticism that ethnographic practitioner research lacks rigour. It follows that, as the political is inextricably part of the research process, there should be a greater onus placed upon practitioner researchers supported by mentors to ensure that analytic procedures are explicit, valid, reliable, and trustworthy.

An inductive approach can test a range of skills; as one practitioner researcher comments:

> *A major problem was the volume of data. . . which overwhelmed me. I learned a hard lesson that preconceived ideas did not work with this method of research. There was a temptation to interpret the data more positively in the light of the study's aim. I had to accept that although I was going to achieve the aim of the study it was not in the way that I had thought.*

Being led by the data is a central element of qualitative approaches. Categories are helpful in teasing out the meaning of findings, with such categories being supported by the data leading to the development of themes. The aim is to create analytical discourses by looking at regularities or variations and seeing how these themes might be connected. There is an interplay of effect and cognition related to how people feel and what they learn as they go about the messy business of 'doing research'.

Strategies, tactics and consequences

However, the findings from research projects may not be what agencies are looking for or expect. Practitioner researchers may need mentoring support in order to anticipate and manage the dilemma of negative and hostile response from employers. One student commented:

> *Because of the damning nature of the findings of this study, I feel reluctant to present the full findings to my colleagues.*

Dissemination of research can become intensely political to the extent that employers could request that their employees withdraw from the research if they are at odds with the findings of the project. Intervention by tutorial staff may be necessary in order to minimise distress to the student and to offer alternative strategies to manage 'the problem'. It is important that practitioner research is carried out sensitively and ethically and that permission and advice of relevant ethics committees are sought. However, it may not be possible to account for the political sensitivities of every workplace. One tried and tested way is to ensure that confidentiality is maintained and to remind those involved that the resultant dissertation is primarily for the award of an MSc degree to a particular individual. If the agency wishes to access research by employees, this can be managed by the preparation of a report which covers the main findings. This in our experience has worked for the parties concerned and often led to partnerships with agencies based on a growing appreciation of the value of the research completed by their employees.

Conclusion
The world of care in the community is bound up with both the political and the personal. It involves people who engage in that world acting as users, carers, professionals in health and social care, and also as teachers and researchers. The actors may play all or some of those roles concurrently or sequentially. The links between the personal and the political in welfare can be subtle, at times both embraced or critiqued. This chapter has sought to make sense of some of this world by contextualising the experiences of practitioner researchers whose 'day job' is to work as practitioners or managers in community care.

There is evidence to support the view that social work is inevitably a political intervention (Payne 1996) and social workers play a significant part in the intensely large 'P' political world of community care. Payne (1996) comments that social work interaction processes and problem solving are analogous to the learning process in higher education and indeed that social work processes can be understood by seeing parallels between the two. This echoes our experience with practitioner researchers undertaking qualitative research work into community care. To take this a stage further it would be legitimate, based on the empirical evidence presented, to argue that the political and the personal are linked in qualitative practitioner research in a way that can be significant for the individual researcher's personal development and also offer fresh insights into the world of community care for agencies' research and development agendas. Usually through the undertaking, supervising or managing of research comes a greater understanding of the dynamics of power and strategies for redressing imbalances.

Both practitioner researchers and their agencies may be wary and defensive about research that is perceived as 'political'. To acknowledge the potential pitfalls and to argue for competence in research activity are one important and necessary way of dealing with this situation. Employer agencies, assisted by three-way learning contracts between the practitioner researcher, the organisation manager, and the research supervisor, could make stronger links between performance review, staff development, and policy formation. This could enhance agency aims and policy implementation, as well as practitioner's training, research, and management/career agendas. Most agencies need to move from a *row* to a *steer* approach, the latter harnessing the strengths, and possibly even the research products and research-based ideas, of their workforce. Credible research accounts that represent a more subtle 'under the surface' view about the world of community care have a direct bearing on social policy formation, for those willing to listen. Unfortunately, a more common picture is that a practitioner researcher returns to the agency 'fired up' with enthusiasm, ready to offer insights into service developments and policy formation, only to find that their work is not valued or even acknowledged. Perhaps this is a sad reflection of the times reinforced by the realities of competition rather than partnership.

It has been argued here that there is still a long way to go in closing the gaps between the practice wisdom generated from practitioner research and the application of the *outcomes* of such research in agencies. It is important to question the assumed value of 'scientific' approaches to research *vis-á-vis* qualitative practitioner research. To assume that qualitative practitioner research is less rigorous or less 'trustworthy' than more-positivist approaches is to ignore the significance and contribution of practice theory. Practice knowledge does not normally accumulate in an absolute sense, but is grounded, and grows and changes through an evolving dialectical process. It is this author's contention that practitioner research using qualitative methods be accorded greater recognition as an approach and method than seems to be the case. Conducted with rigour, and proper supervision, qualitative research in community care illuminates and informs the contested areas within policy and practice in community care in invaluable ways.

References:

Ball, S. J. (1990) *Politics and Policy Making in Education* London, Routledge,

Broad, B., Fletcher, C. (eds.) (1993) *Practitioner Social Work Research In Action* London, Whiting and Birch.

Ely, M., Anzull, M., Friedman,T., Garner, D., McCormack, A. (1991) *Doing Qualitative Research: Circles within Circles* London, Steinmetz Falmer Press,

Finch, J. (1984) 'It's great to have someone to talk to: the ethics and politics of interviewing women' in Bell, C. and Roberts, H. (eds.) *Social Researching, Politics, Problems, Practice* London, Routledge and Kegan Paul, 70-87.

Freire, P. (1972) *Pedagogy of the Oppressed* London, Harmondsworth Penguin.

Gorman, H. (1996) 'Sinking or swimming, has anyone got a liferaft? Care managers and decision making in community care' in Parker, M. (ed.) *Ethics and Community, proceedings of the 1995 conference of the Centre of Professional Ethics*, University of Central Lancashire, 200-12.

Gorman, H., Gurney, A., Harvey, A., Hutchinson, O., Sylvester, V. and Warburton, O. (1996). 'The value of analysing the interlocking nature of oppression for those engaged in working and learning together in community care'. *Journal of Interprofessional Care*, Vol.10, No.2, 1996,147-57.

Halmos, P. (1978) *The Personal and the Political* London, Hutchinson.

Johnson,T. (1972) *Professions and Power* London, Macmillan.

Lincoln, Y. S. and Guba, E. G. (1985) *Naturalistic Inquiry*. Beverley Hills, Calif. Sage.

McGrath, M. (1996) 'The Care Managers' role: issues in implementation.' Paper presented at The Way Forward for Community Care Conference. London, 3 July 1996.

Oakley, A. (1981) 'Interviewing women: a contradiction in terms' in Roberts, H. (ed.) *Doing Feminist Research* London, Routledge and Kegan Paul, 30-62.

Oppenheim, A. N. (1992) *Questionnaire Design, Interviewing and Attitude Measurement* London, New Edition Pinter.

Payne, M. (1996) *What is Professional Social Work?* Birmingham,Venture Press.

Perlmutter, H. and Trist, E. (1986) *Paradigms for Societal Transition* London, Tavistock.

Scott, D. and Usher, R. (eds.) (1996) *Understanding Educational Research* London, Routledge.

Simms, M. (1989) 'Social Research and the Rationalisation of Care' in Gubrium, J and Silverman, D (eds.) *The Politics of Field Research* (1989) London, Sage,173-97.

Stares, A. L. (1987) *Qualitative Analysis for Social Scientists* Cambridge, Cambridge University Press.

Wilkes, R. (1981) *Social Work with Undervalued Groups* London,Tavistock.

Wilson, G. (1996) *Community Care Asking the Users* London, Chapman Hall.

Notes on contributors

Bob Broad is a Senior Research Fellow in the Department of Social and Community Studies at De Montfort University, Leicester. He has previously been a social worker lecturer at the London School of Economics and Science, a probation officer in inner London, and worked in senior child care management. His research interests span child care, young people, family support, and criminal justice areas. His book *Punishment Under Pressure: The Probation Service in the Inner City,* based on his PhD study, was published by Jessica Kingsley Publishers (London) in 1991, and he co-edited (with Colin Fletcher) the book *Practitioner Social Work Research in Action* published in 1993. His last book, *Young People Leaving Care: Life after the Children Act 1989* was published in 1998 by Jessica Kingsley.

Louise Brown is manager of a research partnership formed between the University of Bath and Wiltshire Social Services Department. The research unit specialise in evaluating new developments and practice initiatives for both the child care and adult care divisions in social services. Wiltshire have a particular interest in developments around the health and social care interface and the impact of Family Group Conferences in child protection work. Louise has a background in child protection social work in both the voluntary and statutory sectors, leaving practice in 1972 to follow an interest in 'what works' in social work. Her interests now are in promoting an evidence base for social services through the design of good quality, rigorous research projects..

Kusminder Chahal is a Research Fellow in the Health and Ethnicity Unit at the University of Central Lancashire. He has eight years research experience and has undertaken projects with both black and white communities in a variety of areas – including health, community needs analysis, trade union activity. He is currently undertaking a Joseph Rowntree Foundation funded research project on Racial Harassment and Attacks in the UK investigating the consequences and impact of racist victimisation.

Mike Fisher is Professor and Director of Research at the National Institute for Social Work (London UK) where he directs two Department of Health funded programmes of research into community care and the social services workforce. He is a qualified social worker and has experience of teaching and research in social work at three UK universities.

Helen Gorman has been Course Director of the MSc in Collaborative Community Care at the University of Central England in Birmingham since 1992. Prior to that she worked in further education at the former Birmingham Polytechnic, was responsible for the CQSW element of BA Sociology (Social Work). A law graduate, qualified social worker and ASW, she has worked in juvenile justice, generic social work and as a GP liaison social worker. She has acted as consultant to a range of community care training initiatives and is a member of a FENCE European project on community care curricula. Her research is on the role of the care manager and changing professional identity.

Jennifer Harris is Principal Lecturer (Research) in the Department of Social Work, University of Central Lancashire. Her career has incorporated a variety of paid and voluntary work within the social work field including integrating disabled children within mainstream education. She took a degree in social work and CQSW at Lancaster University and during this period developed a specialisation in work with Deaf people. Jennifer was awarded a PhD in Social Policy in 1994 from Lancaster University for her thesis entitled *The Cultural Meaning of Deafness* (Avebury, 1995). Her second book *Deafness and the Hearing* was published by Venture Press (1997). Her research interests are qualitative methodology, disability studies, parasuicide, and cultural difference.

Mark Harrison is Director of the Centre for Social Action, DeMontfort University, Leicester and has been involved in the development of social action since its earliest days in the 1970s. He has 17 years' youth and community work experience, working for some time at Nottingham Youth Volunteers developing social action groupwork with young people at risk and in trouble. He has undertaken a wide range of consultancy and project development work including a health needs assessment in Derby, a feasibility study for Barnardo's and youth crime prevention projects in Bradford. He helped to establish the young homeless projects London Connection and Resettlement Centre in Birmingham and has also been a consultant on a housing feasibility study for Praxis, a voluntary agency working with refugees in London. Mark's extensive training experience includes running training courses on social action youth work, groupwork, and the Children Act 1989. He is currently part of the Centre's team which is engaged with training governmental and non-governmental agencies in Russia and Ukraine.

Debra Hayes is a senior lecturer in the Department of Applied Community Studies at Manchester Metropolitan University. Her social work experience is largely rooted in criminal justice work: it was here that she began to develop her research interest in immigration and deportation issues. She has recently completed a research project in conjunction with the immigration aid unit in Manchester concerning health and immigration.

Beth Humphries is a principal lecturer in the Department of Applied Community Studies at Manchester Metropolitan University. She has worked in statutory and voluntary social work and has carried out research on a number of social work topics. She has written articles on research and social work education, and is editor of *Critical Perspectives on Empowerment*, published in 1996 by Venture Press.

Lisa Loveridge's pre-qualification social work experience was with homeless people with learning disabilities in both voluntary and statutory residential and day care settings. She graduated from Bath University in 1995 with a Degree in Sociology and Social Work and a Diploma in Social Work, specialising in community care. Her dissertation was an original evaluation of a voluntary sector project which provides therapeutic day care for people with severe mental health difficulties. After qualifying she worked part time as a social worker with physically disabled adults and spent 18 months as a part-time research associate in the Department of Nursing at Birmingham University. This involved evaluating two general hospitals (mainly by setting up a database to act as a patients records system and a tool for research). She is now practising social work with adults who have learning difficulties in Bath.

Ian Paylor PhD has had a wide research experience in a number of settings. His current research interests include undertaking a large-scale crime survey in Cumbria. Previous research has concerned: other crime surveys; an evaluation of a project designed to assist unemployed young males; evaluation of youth workers' practice; provision of legal services; evaluation of change within a social services department; the needs and problems of seasonal workers; social work and young offenders; assessing older adults' numerical skills; understanding change in a family centre; and the experiences of men and women leaving prison. In 1994-5 he was a member of a successful Rowntree funded research team which studied job satisfaction and dissatisfaction amongst residential care workers.

Caroline McGee is a Research Officer with the National Society for the Prevention of Cruelty to Children. She currently leads a long-term research project funded by the BBC Children in Need Appeal looking at 'Children's and Mother's Experiences of Child Protection Following Domestic Violence'. Her research experience includes a fellowship with University Galaway Ireland and she is currently carrying out research on sexual violence for a part-time PhD at Birkbeck College, University of London.

Maria Ruegger is a Senior Lecturer in Social Work at De Montfort University. She is also a Guardian ad Litem on the Hertfordshire Panel Guardians ad Litem and Reporting Officers. She qualified as a special worker in 1978 and worked in the fields of mental health and child care. Since 1985 when she took up a teaching post at the university she has maintained strong links with practice both as an independent social worker and as a guardian ad litem. Her recent research interests include Children's Perspectives of the Guardian ad Litem Service and Mentoring in General Practice.

Ian Shaw is Director of Research in the School of Social and Administrative Studies, University of Wales, Cardiff. He is a social worker who teaches, researches and writes about practice evaluation, qualitative methodology, homelessness, prostitution, and professional decision making. His recent work has led to *Housing and Social Care* with Susan and David Clapham, 1998, Jessica Kingsley; a text on *Qualitative Evaluation*, Sage, and an edited collection, with Joyce Lishman, of 'state of play' papers on *Evaluation and Social Work Practice*, Sage. He is also responsible for the development of a forthcoming bilingual (Welsh and English / English only) computer assisted learning course of core social, work competencies.

Carole Truman is a Lecturer in Applied Social Science and a member of the Institute for Women's Studies at Lancaster University. She is co-editor (with Beth Humphries and Donna Mertens) of *Research in an Unequal World* (UCL Press, forthcoming) and (with Beth Humphries) *Re-thinking Social Research* (Avebury, 1994). She has a long-standing interest in the relationship of social research to marginalised groups. She is currently Project Director of a study exploring violence, sexuality and space, which focuses on homophobic violence and the creation of safe social spaces.